Anonymous

Albert Memorial Guide Book to Edinburgh and its Environs

Anonymous

Albert Memorial Guide Book to Edinburgh and its Environs

ISBN/EAN: 9783337180645

Printed in Europe, USA, Canada, Australia, Japan

Cover: Foto ©ninafisch / pixelio.de

More available books at **www.hansebooks.com**

Messrs James Middlemass & Co had the honour of presenting Two Copies of this Guide to Edinburgh to Her Majesty the Queen, and have received the following letter from the late Lieut. General Sir T. M. Biddulph,

Albert Memorial

Inaugurated by Her Majesty, Queen Victoria,

at Edinburgh, 17th August, 1876.

Albert Memorial Guide Book to Edinburgh

AND

ITS ENVIRONS

EDINBURGH.

JAMES MIDDLEMASS & CO. 18 SOUTH BRIDGE.

ENTERED AT STATIONERS HALL.

James Middlemass & Co., 18 South Bridge, Edinburgh.

DEAR SIRS,—In answer to your inquiry regarding the Clothing with which you have supplied me, I have to state that it is in every respect satisfactory.

The various garments fit well, and I have no doubt will give satisfaction in wearing.

I shall be glad to recommend any of my friends in America who may intend visiting Scotland, to call at your Establishment, and get supplied with any Clothing they may require.—I am, DEAR SIRS, yours very faithfully,

E. R. BEADLE.

EDINBURGH, 10th July, 1877.

GENTLEMEN,—I thank you very sincerely for kindness in forwarding my portmanteau to Glasgow, and for all the other services which you have so promptly rendered me.

I am glad that I waited until I reached Edinburgh before procuring the Clothing which I required, as the quality of the cloth which you have given me is evidently of great excellence. I like the shade very much, and the fit is all that I could desire.

The suit of Athol cloth, and the heavy outside coat for winter wear, could not be excelled, and I wish that all my friends in Philadelphia were similarly provided. I shall take care to advise all friends and tourists whom I may know, to follow my course in crossing the Atlantic, if they take Edinburgh in their way. I burdened myself with no stock of raiment on leaving home, as I knew that at your place of business I could procure all I wanted, and that of the best and most enduring quality.

Again thanking you for your great kindness,—I am, GENTLEMEN, most sincerely yours,

WILLIAM BLACKWOOD.

EDINBURGH, 17th July, 1877.

DEAR SIRS,—When in your city in 1874, I purchased from you a good supply of Clothing, and after the wearing of three years have found it to give entire satisfaction in every respect. As a proof of my confidence in your work and goods, and the reasonableness of your terms, I have just ordered a fresh supply, which will last for two or three years to come. I do most cordially commend your House to the notice and patronage of my American friends who may be visiting Edinburgh and Scotland.—Yours sincerely,

DAVID A. CUNNINGHAM.

EDINBURGH, 6th July, 1877.

James Middlemass & Co., 18 South Bridge, Edinburgh.

The following is a List of American and Canadian Gentlemen with whom we have had business transactions. Strangers to the Establishment will have no difficulty in getting information as to how they have been satisfied. (See also Letters, pp. 1, 2.)

Rev. Dr. CUYLER, New York.
E. M. JENKINS, Esq., New York.
J. E. COLVILLE, Esq., Stapleton, New York.
Rev. Dr. MURPHY, Philadelphia.
Rev. JOSEPH BEGGS, Philadelphia.
WM. J. HOLMES, Esq., Canada.
JAMES M. SMITH, Esq., Boston.
Rev. JAMES DINSMORE, Kentucky.
LEWIS W. SMITH, Esq., Philadelphia.
F. C. BRIGGS, Esq., Boston.
A. H. BROWN, Esq., Washington.
Dr. H. A. HAGEN, Cambridge, Mass.
Dr. NORRIS, Cambridge, Mass.
Dr. G. M'LEAN, Chicago.
A. J. LOECHER, Esq., Philadelphia.
PHILO A. OTIS, Esq., Chicago.
JOHN L. BLAIKIE, Esq., Toronto.
F. H. PIERCE, Esq., New Hampshire.
W. H. SMITH, Esq., New York.
E. M. FURMAN, Esq., New York.
Captain F. SAUNDERS, Lynchburg, Va.
Rev. A. G. RULIFFSON, New York.
T. D. WITHERSPOON, Esq., Va.
Rev. GILES B. COOKE, Petersburgh, Va.
R. H. WILLIS, Esq., Norwood, Va.
Professor BARNARD, Vermont.
JOHN A. TANNER, Esq., Virginia.
J. E. WOOD, Esq., Gloversville.
A. TERWILLIGER, Esq., Preble.
P. GIBSON, Esq., Cincinnati.
Rev. J. A. WILLIAMS, Baltimore.
THOMAS KENNEDY, Esq., Brooklyn.
GEORGE J. ABBOT, Esq., Meadville.
Rev. A. A. LIVERMORE, Meadville.
H. J. WOLCOTT, Esq., Newhaven.
CHARLES WOLCOTT, Esq., Fishkill on Hudson.
JOHN MACNAB, Esq., Eaufaula, Ala.
WM. HOWDEN, Esq., San Francisco.
Rev. Dr. FAIRBAIRN, Annandale, N.Y.
Rev. W. GRANT, Vanlaach Hill, Canada.
Hon. F. MOREY, Louisiana.
Rev. T. WALDEN, Boston.
LUCIUS HOPKINS, Esq., New York.
JUDAH FRISBIE, Esq., Newhaven.
J. M. GAZZAM, Esq., Pittsburgh.
Colonel R. D. MITCHELL, New Orleans.
F. H. CAMP, Esq., Watertown.
Rev. W. R. BROWN, Leavenworth, Kansas.
Rev. Mr. FAIRFIELD, Mansfield, Ohio.
WALDO HUTCHINS, Jun., Esq., N.Y.
THOMAS MORRELL, Esq., New York.
Dr. N. L. SNOW, Canjoharrie, New York.
ROBERT BUIST, Jun., Esq., Philadelphia.
Dr. J. S. COHEN, Philadelphia.
W. H. MORRELL, Esq., New York.
DAVID BAKER, Esq., New York.
Dr. COLVILLE, New York.
R. HUTCHISON, Esq., Newark, N.J.
J. WAYMAN, Esq., Chicago.
JOHN CRERAR, Esq., Chicago.
W. F. CRAFTS, Esq., Haveral, Mass.
JOHN INGLIS, Esq., New York.
L. T. DICKSON, Esq., Philadelphia.
J. A. FOSTER, Esq., South Carolina.
Rev. WM. PORTER, Beloit, Wisconsin.
Rev. Mr. LAURIE, Providence.
Rev. D. STUART, Canada.
GEORGE BARRON, Esq., Chicago.
CHAPMAN FREEMAN, Esq., Philadel.
JOHN DUNCAN, Esq., Washington.
T. N. CREAM, Esq., Levis, Canada.
THOMAS INGLIS, Esq., Chicago.
A. M'DONALD, Esq., Lynchburg, Va.
JOHN M'KINLAY, Esq., New York.
Rev. B. F. HAYES, Lewiston, Maine.
ED. TUCKERMAN, Esq., Amhurst, Massachusetts.
DAVID BEVERIDGE, Esq., Chicago.
JAMES INGLIS, Esq., Montreal, Canada.
Dr. VANDERPOEL, New York.
C. G. TURNBULL, Esq., St. John's, N.B.
CHARLES S. RHINELANDER, Esq., New York.
J. B. WATSON, Esq., Troy, New York.
Dr. THOMPSON, New York.
FRANK PRINGLE, Esq., New York.
D. SAGE, Esq., 67 Wall Street, New York.
CHAS. R. KING, Esq., Philadelphia.
JAMES J. DUNCAN, Esq., New York.
Dr. EUGENE SMITH, Detroit, Mich.
CHAS. GEO. COLVILLE, Esq., N. York.
Professor LYALL, Halifax.
Rev. Dr. CUNNINGHAM, Philadelphia.
GEO. PENDREIGH, Esq., New York.
Rev. Dr. ROCKWELL, Staten Island, New York.
Rev. JOHN EWING, Clinton, New Jer.
J. C. REEVE, Esq., Dayton, Ohio.
E. MEYER, Esq., New York.
E. W. DEAN, Esq., New York.
A. HALLIDAY, Esq., New York.
JAMES E. WOODRUFF, Esq., Quincy, Illinois.
JOHN F. STOER, Esq., Philadelphia

James Middlemass & Co., 18 South Bridge, Edinburgh.

JOSEPH PLATT, Jun., Esq., Waterford, New York.
Dr. D. W. NIXON, Albany, New York.
ROSEWELL SMITH, Esq.
W. KENT, Esq., Pittsburg.
A. MAJORS, Esq., 18 Wall St., New York.
A. HOPKINS, Esq., New Jersey.
J. H. LODER, Esq., Philadelphia.
Rev. H. C. MABIE, Indianapolis.
Mrs. M'BEAN, Chicago.
Mrs. GRAY, Chicago.
H. T. BLAKE, Esq., Newhaven, Conn.
J. B. FRASER, Esq., Upper Ottawa, Canada.
F. W. CROSBY, Esq., 283 Ontario Street, Chicago.
Rev. W. F. BLACKMAN, Ohio.
Rev. J. W. METCALFE, Columbus, Ohio.
Rev. L. H. KING, Pratsville, New York.
F. BRENTON, Esq., Philadelphia.
J. C. PLATT, Esq., Scvanton, Penn.
Dr. SHEARER, Baltimore.
A. M. MUNN, Esq.
B. D. WOOD, Esq., Contractor, New Orleans.
Rev. JAMES RAMSAY, New York.
F. DICKSON, Esq., Cortland Street, N.Y.
JUDSON SMITH, Esq., Oberlin, Ohio.
C. A. MACDONALD, Esq., Chicago.
H. B. PLATT, Esq., New York.
W. LAUDER, Esq., Pennsylvania.
Dr. EMERSON WARNER, 574 Main Street, Worcester, Massachusetts.
R. W. FORLONG, Esq., Lachute, Canada, East.
C. G. BARRETT, Esq., 25 Park Avenue, New York.
Rev. E. P. FARNHAM, Younkers, N.Y.
Rev. G. BULLEN, Pantucket, Rhode Is.
Rev. C. T. BERRY, Caldwell, New Jersey.
W. J. RICHARDSON, Esq., Brooklyn, New York.
S. A. BLATCHFORD, Esq., 29 Nassau Street, New York.
H. ROGER, Esq., Portland, Oregon, U.S.A.
Dr. T. S. ROBERTSON, 28 East Twentieth Street, New York.
GEORGE KENNAN, Esq., 1318 Massachusetts Avenue, Washington.
THOMAS PRINGLE, Esq., Eighteenth and Nineteenth Streets, New York.
A. C. KING, Esq., Detroit, Michigan.
Rev. W. D. ARMSTRONG, Ottawa, Canada.
Sir ALEXANDER GALT, Canada.
JAMES MOORE, Jun., Esq., New York.

Dr. W. H. HARDISON, Richland, Arkansas.
JAMES GOODRICH, Esq., New York.
J. C. HEDDLE, Esq., Chicago.
T. S. PHILLIP, Esq., Chicago.
JAMES WILSON, Esq., Chicago.
Rev. Mr. MACKAY, Pittsburg.
C. B. BAILEY, Esq., New Jersey.
T. C. C. BAILEY, Esq., New Jersey.
Rev. J. KEMPSHILL, Philadelphia.
E. ANTHON, Esq., New York.
ANDREW CARNEGIE, Esq., Pittsburg, Pa.
Rev. R. CAMPBELL, 68 St. Fanville Street, Montreal.
Professor G. C. S. SOUTHWORTH, Kenyon College, Gambier, Ohio.
Rev. Dr. LEFTWICH, Baltimore.
Rev. W. S. BROWN, Reformed Dutch Church, U.S.A.
JOHN DEVLIN, Esq., New York.
Rev. Dr. W. C. R. TAYLOR, Newark, New Jersey.
Rev. Dr. WATERS, 365 Mount Prospect Avenue, New Jersey.
Rev. J. R. JOHNSTONE, Washington, Pennsylvania.
Rev. Dr. BURNS, Halifax, Nova Scotia.
Rev. Dr. KING, Manitoba.
Rev. J. W. FLEMING, Scotch Church, Buenos Ayres, South America.
J. B. KELLOCH, Esq., Boston.
JOSEPH W. SWAIN, Esq., Philadelphia.
Principal CABIN, King's College, Toronto.
Colonel C. S. VENABLE, University of Virginia, U.S.A.
JOHN FIELD, Esq., Market Street, Philadelphia.
B. B. BUCKOUT, Esq., Iowa.
THOMPSON M'COSH, Esq., Burlington, Iowa.
E. W. HAWLEY, Esq., San Francisco.
General WAGER GWAYNE, American Exchange, London.
F. N. DAY, Esq., Stratford, New Hampshire, U.S.A.
W. H. APPLETON, Esq., Philadelphia.
CHARLES BURNHAM, Esq., Globe Theatre, Boston, Massachusetts.
W. B. MEANY, Esq., M.D., St. Louis, U.S.A.
Rev. Dr. BISHOP, Kansas, America.
D. L. WESSON, Esq., N. York and London.
S. J. ANDERSON LAING, Esq., Boston.
T. S. ELY, Esq., New York.
J. B. KELLOCK, Esq., Boston.

JAMES MIDDLEMASS & CO., CLOTHIERS, SHIRT MAKERS, AND OUTFITTERS,
18 SOUTH BRIDGE, EDINBURGH.

The Prince Consort Memorial,

WITH

A BIOGRAPHICAL SKETCH OF HIS ROYAL HIGHNESS.

THE profound grief which spread throughout the land on the death of His Royal Highness the late Prince Consort was so universal that it would be difficult to find words to express it. The whole nation, —Europe, America—indeed, the entire civilised world—shared in the heavy affliction of the Queen and the Royal Family. Perhaps no other death in this country has ever been so keenly felt, no loss so universally regretted. In the very prime of manhood, endowed with an imposing presence, ennobled by the virtue and talents of an accomplished mind, animated with a big and generous heart, and occupying an exalted and favoured station—the beloved husband of our Most Gracious Queen, and the affectionate father of her family,—the Prince was most unexpectedly cut down by the hand of death. The private loss was also a public calamity—not only a severe blow to our Sovereign the Queen, but an irreparable loss to the nation. He was one that had watched over the interests and progress of our industries, and when he went hence he left a sad blank in the councils of our institutions for the promotion and advancement of the Arts and Sciences. Indeed, the Prince Consort has been remembered with a mixture of joy, regret, and tenderness—a lively joy and admiration for the illustrious dead, which flow from the nation's unfeigned love and grateful remembrance of a life so truly good, so really useful; a regret that so diligent a worker in the midst of the refined activities and practical forces of our industries should have been so early removed from amongst us; and a tenderness and heartfelt sympathy for the suffering and sorrowing widow and Royal Household. Out of this great love and admiration of Scotland for one whose large heart was ever with the people in all well-doing, came the hearty resolution to pay a suitable and national tribute to the memory of the Prince. Shortly after the lamentable death of His Royal Highness, steps were taken to realise this laudable object and desire of all classes of the people, resulting in a magnificent production of art, which discovers a power of conception and a wonderful purity of treatment in execution, not surpassed by any monument of the kind in ancient, mediæval, or modern sculpture. For this national tribute to departed worth above thirty designs were publicly exhibited at the Royal Institution. A Committee of Advice, of the most competent judges in art, most attentively examined the sketches, which were from the pencils of our most eminent artists, and weighed the general opinion of most distinguished visitors, and having honestly applied their own judgment, selected six of the most meritorious of the designs, and submitted them for Her Majesty's decision. It need scarcely be added, that real merit in completeness of conception, in so far as an illustrative and instructive memorial of the life of the Prince Consort was the leading idea, was the guiding principle in the choice of the Committee of Advice. Not only a graceful and harmonious composition, but, as we have already said, an illustrative and instructive monument, was steadily kept in view by the Queen in giving her decision. It speaks much for Her Majesty's judgment and good taste to know that Sir Charles Eastlake, then President of the Royal Academy, confirmed the Queen's decision without having had the slightest hint of Her Majesty's choice, which gave a preference to a design by Mr. John Steell, R.S.A.

The Memorial.

We may say at once that this great pyramidal monument of the late Prince Consort is not only the *chef-d'œuvre* of our Scottish sculptor Mr. Steell, but unmistakably the greatest and most expressive realisation of life in art of any monumental design in Great Britain. The equestrian statue itself, entirely the work of the designer, independent of the subordinate groups, discovers, as we have already said, a power of conception and execution scarcely surpassed by the old or modern school of art. The design, as a whole, is thoroughly artistic and graphically illustrative. The attitude of the Prince is graceful and dignified, yet easy and natural, exhibiting at a glance the noble bearing of the hereditary Prince, and of the accomplished gentleman, imbued with a catholic spirit and with the high and honourable principles that pervaded every part of his public and private life. The features of the Prince possess depth of feeling and grace, and the life-expression is most striking—a marvellous likeness indeed, which has received the unqualified approbation of Her Majesty. His Royal Highness sits erect in the saddle, with head uncovered, in military costume. His right hand hangs straight by his side, holding gracefully his plumed hat, as if he had just returned a courteous salutation. The left hand is clear of the figure, and is in the position of quietly governing the movements of the massive but high-spirited charger. Horse and rider evidently understand one another. This centre feature of the Memorial has boldness of conception, yet is perfectly subdued by the happy expression of the benignant countenance of the Prince, and the quiet attitude of rest of the high-mettled charger. The horse, although standing on all fours, appears to be full of courage and strength,—" a noble steed, that looks as if the speed of thought were in his limbs." In the subordinate groups, the "sweet charities" of life, even to every minor detail, find expression, and the joys, affections, and duties of life are portrayed without the least affectation. In fact, in a sentence, we may describe the surrounding subsidiary gatherings as so many historic groups of actors within the shade of a magnificent scenic setting, the whole forming a gorgeous and instructive representation of a truly national drama, that brings out in one harmonious composition of art the usefulness and domestic life and exalted dignity and duties of our beloved Queen's husband, and the President of the Great Exhibition of Industry of all Nations, of 1851. It is the most remarkable production of genius in Scotland, as it is certainly the most expressive and instructive monument of a short but illustrious life, embellished by the spotless virtues and the talents of an exalted nature. This great conception of Mr. Steell enables a people to realise more fully the peaceful but eminently useful career of the good Prince Consort, who has passed away from amongst us, but has left a valuable legacy to all men and nations in the beautiful impress of a life that was entirely devoted to the intellectual training and the welfare of the great brotherhood of civilisation.

Biographical Sketch.

Francis-Albert-Augustus-Charles-Emmanuel, Duke of Saxe-Coburg-Gotha, and Prince Consort of our beloved Sovereign Queen Victoria, was born at Rosenau, near Coburg, on the 26th August 1819, and died at Windsor Castle, 14th December 1861. His Royal Highness was the second son of the late Duke of Saxe-Coburg-Gotha, and was carefully educated along with his elder brother. The Prince attended the University of Bonn from May 1837 to September 1838, where, in addition to the science of government and the art of legislation, he received instruction in the study of abstract science in its relation to the progress of industry. The schools and universities of the whole of Germany are much devoted to the study of the abstract sciences for the promotion of the industrial arts, and thus the young Duke reaped all the advantages of the teaching of his native country in those fields of research and observation that have produced the intellectual element in the productions of the Continent. The technical classes of Germany very efficiently prepared the young Prince in carrying out the idea of Mr. F. Whishaw, Secretary of the Society of Arts in 1844, for a Great Exhibition of Industry, which, through the unwearied exertions and advocacy of the Prince Consort in 1849, was actually accomplished two years afterwards. At the University of Bonn, the Prince also devoted himself with ardour to the study of natural history and chemistry, which lead intimately to a knowledge of geology and the arts. Habits of observation are the first fruits of the Continental system of technical instruction, and hence we had in his late Royal Highness a most fitting President of the Great Exhibition of 1851. It was early discovered by his teachers that this noble scion of the House of Saxe-Coburg-Gotha was passionately fond of painting and music, the latter of which was cultivated during his whole residence in England. Several compositions of the Prince obtained publicity in this country, and one of his operas was performed after his death in London. The Prince visited England in 1838-39, and was naturalised as a subject of Great Britain, 24th January 1840. On his marriage, Prince Albert received the title of Royal Highness, and obtained the rank of Field-Marshal, the knighthood of the Order of the Bath, and the command of a regiment of Hussars. The imposing ceremony of the marriage took place at St. James's Palace, 10th February 1840. In 1842, the title of Consort was conferred upon him, and that of Prince Consort by letters patent under the Great Seal on the 25th June 1857. His Royal Highness also succeeded to many other offices of the highest distinction in the kingdom. He was admitted a member of the Privy Council, made Governor and Constable of Windsor Castle, was elected Chancellor of the University of Cambridge, 28th February 1847, and became Master of Trinity House. His reply to Viscount Canning and the other Commissioners of the Great Exhibition, as the President of that great undertaking, is a chaste and elegant piece of composition, based upon the touching and beautiful passage—

> "The earth is the Lord's, and the fulness thereof,
> The compass of the world, and they that dwell therein."

It is to the honour of the memory of this distinguished and accomplished Prince, that notwithstanding his exalted position as a member of the Privy Council, and husband of the Sovereign, he was never known to have interfered at all with State affairs, nor in any way to attempt to use his high and great influence with political sections of the Government or the country. A wise and rare prudence and tact characterised his whole public career. He possessed a perfect insight of his duties arising from so favoured a position; and with an exact and complete knowledge of the growth of political liberty in England, the Prince Consort ever steered clear of the petty jealousy and annoying detraction of parties. Admired by all for his wisdom, beloved for his virtue, and sought after only as a diligent worker and helper on the great highway of human progress, the Prince moved out and in amongst us with a spotless reputation for all that was good, beautiful, and true. His eminent services as the promoter and President of the first Exhibition were recognised by the memorial statue of the Prince by Mr. Joseph Durham, which was commenced immediately after the closing of the great gathering of all nations, and placed in the Gardens of the Royal Horticultural Society, and uncovered in the presence of the Prince and Princess of Wales, 10th June 1863.

In truth, the history of the Great Exhibition brings out at once the energy of the late Prince Consort. The original idea of a National Exhibition, as we have already noticed, is due to Mr. F. Whishaw, Secretary of the Society of Arts in 1844. It was not taken up, however, till 1849, when Prince Albert, President of the Society, said, "Now is the time to prepare for a great exhibition, an exhibition worthy of the greatness of this country, not merely national in its scope but comprehensive of the whole world; and I offer myself to the public as their leader, if they are willing to assist in the undertaking." These noble and generous sentiments were at once responded to, and the Royal Commission was appointed, 1850. Paxton then designed *The Crystal Palace*, and the building was begun in the same year. Thus the idea of Whishaw in 1844, carried out by his Royal Highness in 1849, bore fruit in 1851.

At the Prince's death, four sons and five daughters composed the Royal Family The eldest, the Princess-Royal Victoria, was born 21st November 1840, and Princess Beatrice, the youngest, was born 14th April 1857. In one of the subordinate groups of the Memorial which faces the south, the happy home of our Sovereign is seen illustrated as it existed during the life-time of the Prince Consort. This is certainly the most interesting group of the whole composition. It comprises expressive and beautifully-executed likenesses of the young members of the Royal House. The tenderness and living light of parental affection mingle with the innocent glow of childhood. The sunshine and sainted love of the mother fall upon the features of the infant Princess Beatrice in her lap, and the dreamings of future life and action nestle on the finely-chiselled forehead of our Sailor Prince. The illustrious father sits by the side of the Queen with book in hand, and the little Prince Leopold and Princess Louise are standing at his knee watching every look and smile of the loving parent. Other members of the Royal Family are present in conversation, and thus, in this sweet group of domestic life, we have an insight of the Royal Home of England in the days of the Prince Consort.

Inauguration of the Memorial.

All the more important arrangements for the ceremonial of the inauguration of the Prince Consort Memorial on Thursday the 17th August 1876 had been announced weeks previously to that date; and when, on the morning of Wednesday the 16th, the guns boomed a salute of welcome from the Castle, the citizens knew that the Queen had arrived, and that the programme, which had been drawn up with so much pleasant anticipation, was now about to be carried out. Meantime the decorations on the route from Holyrood Palace to and from Charlotte Square, in the centre of which the Memorial had been raised, were all but completed, and the city was already *en fête*. Never did Edinburgh look gayer, brighter, more beautiful, than on the day of Her Majesty's arrival here to unveil the monument raised in honour of her illustrious husband. The "grey Metropolis of the North" had thrown aside what is supposed to be her usual sober livery. The summer of the South seemed to have settled over her "palaces and towers;" and her hills and rocks, the singular antique pile of her Old, and the white streets and crescents of her New Town, her gardens in the heart of the city, her citadel, with its cloud-swept towers, rising from foundations rooted in a wooded vale, all gleamed in sunshine, and displayed that strength and variety of colour which the brightness of "Queen's weather" never fails to call forth. It will long remain a pleasant recollection in Edinburgh that Her Majesty, on the occasion of this her latest visit, had an opportunity of seeing the city and its picturesque suburbs at their best and brightest. The Royal Lady, who had come direct from Osborne, had been travelling all night by train, and after a brief rest had received an important deputation of the members of the Corporation; yet she was not deterred by the fatigues of the journey or of the civic interview from driving out in the evening in search of the enjoyment and solace which picturesque scenery never fails to afford her. At six in the evening, Her Majesty, accompanied by Princess Beatrice and suite, drove out from Holyrood Palace into the city by the chief eastern approach, which affords magnificent views of Arthur Seat and the Salisbury Crags on the left, and of Calton Hill on the right. Proceeding by Abbey Hill, Regent Road, and Waterloo Place, the Royal party were readily recognised in Princes Street, and received there with the most loyal, if not the most noisy, demonstrations. Thence the route was through Princes Street, along the Dean Bridge and Queensferry Road, past Cramond, and through the grounds of Dalmeny House, the residence of the Earl of Rosebery. The journey was continued until, passing Barnbougle Castle, an ascent was reached, from which North Queensferry and the upper reaches of the Firth of Forth, jewelled with islets, were revealed. During the outward journey, the westering sun had added all the charm to the scenes through which Her Majesty passed that high summer sunshine can confer upon essentially noble scenery; and when the remote and silent islets of the upper Firth, and the ancient ferry over which the Scottish queens were wont to cross to "Dunfermline toun" came into view, a pause was made, the horses' heads were turned, and then homewards to Holyrood the Royal party rode, with the sunset covering the Forth with a gold enamel, and lighting up the hills of Fife with the lustre of amethyst

On the following day, the day of the inauguration of the Memorial, the weather was unpromising. About noon however, the air became clearer, and as the time for the starting of the procession approached, the weather became fine. A slight haze veiled the sunlight, and the heat which had prevailed on the previous day was tempered by a pleasant breeze, which, besides being refreshing to the vast crowds that were massed along the line of route, had a value from the picturesque point of view, as in fluttering the numberless bannerets and flags, it immensely enhanced the gaiety of the appearance of the decorations. At about three o'clock, Her Majesty's escort, consisting of one hundred men of the 7th Hussars, under command of His Royal Highness the Duke of Connaught, arrived in the Palace Yard, and formed; and shortly afterwards the Royal party and suite left the Palace in three carriages, the third of which was occupied by Her Majesty, Princess Beatrice, and Prince Leopold. The Queen's carriage, together with those occupied by the ladies and gentlemen in waiting, were each drawn by four horses, with postilions, preceded by outriders. The line of route was guarded by detachments of several regiments and Volunteer corps, and the bands of each corps played the National Anthem as the procession passed. The decorations of private and public buildings, most of them exceedingly tasteful and handsome, consisted generally of hangings of crimson cloth with yellow borders, and enriched with endless figures,—shields, crowns, inscriptions, emblems, flags, &c. Along the whole line of route lofty Venetian masts, covered with crimson cloth, and surmounted with crowns, Prince of Wales' feathers, banners, &c., and connected with lines of dancing bannerets, gave to the successive roads and streets an exceedingly gay appearance. Perhaps no part of the route was more splendidly decorated than George Street, which, with St. Andrew's Square at its east, and Charlotte Square at its west extremity, offered unusual facilities for effective decoration. As the procession moved along this wide thoroughfare, aglow with the crimson draperies of private buildings, and with the scarlet hangings of the platforms and stands,—a long vista of fluttering flags seen extending east and west—the enthusiasm and the loyalty of the vast crowds were expressed in one long continuous cheer as Her Majesty was slowly borne along to the platform and dais that had been prepared for the Royal party in the centre of Charlotte Square, and near the base of the Memorial. The cheering followed Her Majesty to her temporary throne, and then slowly died away, together with the last bars of the music with which the bands within the square welcomed the Queen. There was now a brief period of silence while the ceremony of the inauguration was being performed. The rites were simple, pleasing, and not too imposing to be solemn. Prayer was offered up by one of the Deans of the Chapel Royal; and afterwards a chorale, composed by Prince Albert, was beautifully rendered by Professor Oakeley's choir. Mr. Cross, the Home Secretary, then presented the Executive Committee of the Memorial to Her Majesty, who, after being briefly addressed by the Duke of Buccleuch who sketched the history of the Memorial, read a gracious reply, in which she expressed her appreciation of the affection and admiration of this country for the late Prince Consort, as well as the loyalty and attachment to herself which has ever been the characteristic of her Scottish subjects. Mr. Cross, from his place on the left side of the Queen, proclaimed, in a loud voice, "By Her Majesty's command, I desire that the statue be unveiled." At this moment, by a dexterous movement of his hand, Mr. Steell, the sculptor, who designed the monument, drew a cord which untied a coloured ribband at the top, and immediately, as by magic, the magnificent statue of Prince Albert stood revealed—the new bronze glittering in the subdued lights of the summer sky. One moment the vast crowds filling the square and its avenues gazed at the noble Memorial, and then from all quarters around a hearty cheer arose—the band of the 79th Highlanders struck up the "Coburg March," which had been inserted in the musical programme at Her Majesty's special request—and a royal salute was fired from the Castle. Then followed Professor Oakeley's beautiful chorale, "Evening and Morning," which illustrates the singularly appropriate Scriptural legend, "Weeping may for a night endure; but joy cometh in the morning." The different artists employed on the Memorial—Mr. John Steell, R.S.A., the designer and sculptor; and Mr. William Brodie, R.S.A., Mr. Clark Stanton, A.R.S.A., and Mr. T. W. Stevenson, who executed the subsidiary groups—were then presented to Her Majesty, whose gracious and cordial reception of them showed how highly she appreciated the result of their labours. The Queen, followed by Princess Beatrice, Prince Leopold, and the household in waiting, then walked round the monument, and inspected it from all points, graciously acknowledging the while the cordial cheering which greeted her from all sides. After Professor Oakeley's choir had sung the National Anthem, Her Majesty was conducted to her carriage and drove away amid cheers through the unrivalled thoroughfare of Princes Street down to her classic Palace of Holyrood.

Of the statue itself, which has already been partly described, it is only necessary to say here, that for beauty of design, pleasing proportion, and interesting detail, the Memorial fully merits the high praise already bestowed upon it. The equestrian statue itself is conspicuous for the fine repose and dignity worn lightly, which was one of the most distinguishing characteristics of the Prince Consort—one of the most nobly graceful men of his own or any time. The arrangement of the composition is pyramidal. The equestrian figure is over fourteen feet high, and weighs eight tons; the pedestal is seventeen feet two inches high, and is formed of blocks of Peterhead marble, the largest of them weighing over twenty tons. The artist, Mr. Steell, together with Professor Oakeley, were both summoned to Holyrood, where, in recognition of their genius and services, the Queen conferred upon both the honour of knighthood. Upon Lord Provost Falshaw, who had conducted the principal ceremonies of the inauguration with equal dignity and judgment, a baronetcy was conferred. His Lordship had been introduced to the Queen by Major-General Ponsonby on the arrival of Her Majesty at St. Margaret's Station, and a few hours later, on the occasion of the deputation of the Corporation, Bailies Howden and Methven had been presented to the Queen by the Home Secretary (Mr. Cross) and, together with the Lord Provost, had been permitted to kiss hands. On the evening of the day of the inauguration Her Majesty drove out to Craigmillar Castle. At night, a most picturesque display of coloured limelights and rockets took place in the Queen's Park and or the lower slopes of Arthur's Seat.

After the excitements of the day of the inauguration, Her Majesty spent the morning of the following day almost in privacy. The weather on Friday being oppressively hot the Queen caused tents to be erected in a retired spot of the Palace gardens, and there she spent some time engaged in the transaction of important business of the State. After this Her Majesty amused herself by sketching one or two of the more picturesque views presented by Arthur's Seat and the Crags. During the day Sir John Steell and Sir Herbert Oakeley attended at Holyrood by the Queen's command, and were permitted to inscribe their names in Her Majesty's autograph album; and on the same day Dr. Moffat, the venerable and distinguished African missionary, and the father-in-law of the famous Livingstone, had the honour of an interview with the Queen. In the afternoon the Queen drove out to Dalkeith; and at 11.30 at night Her Majesty left Edinburgh for Balmoral. The scene in the Queen's Park and on the slopes of the hill in the neighbourhood became exceedingly animated and picturesque as the hour for the departure of the Royal Party drew near. It had been arranged that a telling pyrotechnical display should take place at the time of Her Majesty's departure, including a general illumination of the route from Holyrood to St. Margaret's private station by means of variegated lights. The management of the illumination was intrusted to the officials of the Fire Brigade, who stationed their men (each supplied with a torch of coloured fire) at the distance of thirty yards apart, all along the heights from Holyrood to St. Margaret's. The firemen, it was agreed, should all light their torches at a given signal—the firing of a white rocket, which was to be sent up exactly at the moment when the Queen should enter her carriage. Some mistake, however, occurred; the white light was sent up twenty minutes too soon, and the torches were all burned out before the Queen had an opportunity of seeing their effect. Meantime, however, the more adventurous spirits among the great crowd that assembled to witness the Queen's departure had fired the whins on the hill, and created an extempore illumination, wilder and more effective in its running lines of flame and yellow billows of rolling smoke against the dark sky than any display of artificial fires could have been. Thus, amid the festive rejoicings, and with the best wishes of the people of her northern capital, Her Majesty bade adieu to dark Holyrood, to the blazing heights of Arthur's Seat, to the loyal crowds whose cheering greeted her out of the darkness.

Looking back on the occasion and the cause of the Queen's latest visit to Edinburgh, we cannot but regard it as one of the happiest incidents in Her Majesty's reign. The general feeling with regard to it is one of entire satisfaction and grateful remembrance. Although the ceremony was the inauguration of a memorial of the dead, time had so removed the bitterness of remembered loss, that grief had been transformed into sacred content. It was an occasion not of mourning, but of gladness. To the Queen the "lonely splendour" of the Crown was warmed and enriched by the feeling which she so graciously expressed in words, and could not help expressing in looks, that he that had been so long lost to her is dearly remembered, and must ever be regarded with esteem and admiration by her people. To us the day will be remembered with satisfaction, as one of pleasure unshaded by regret or misadventure—as the day on which we saw a happy Queen, and were happy in her happiness. May care never be nearer to her. Meantime, though she is not often amongst us, we have with us the express image and presentment of him in whom her life was centred. From him, as a type of nobleness, we cannot turn.

The Livingstone Monument.

The interesting memorial statue of the late Dr. David Livingstone, of which an engraving is already given, is the latest addition to the series of monuments commemorative of eminent Scotchmen in Princes Street Gardens, and was inaugurated on the 15th August 1876. The name of Livingstone is as familiar as it is highly esteemed in every civilised land, and it is unnecessary here to do more than refer to the life and works of him, who as missionary and explorer in Africa, has achieved more distinction than any predecessor—of him who, after forty years spent in mission labour and geographical discovery in Africa, found a last resting-place in Westminster Abbey. The monument, situated in East Princes Street Gardens, a few yards east of the famous Scott Monument, and near the curve of the Waverley Bridge leading south to the railway station, consists of a striking bronze statue eight feet high, modelled by Mrs. D. O. Hill, and placed upon an artistic pedestal of freestone designed by the sculptor's brother, Sir Noel Paton.

LIVINGSTON,

INAUGURATED AT EDINBURGH 15TH AUGUST, 1876.

Albert Memorial Guide to Edinburgh.

OPINIONS OF THE PRESS.

Edinburgh Courant, 10th April, 1877.

It might have been thought that another guide to Edinburgh was superfluous, but this handsome book just issued by Messrs. James Middlemass & Co. has some features which will cause it to be prized by the tourist and sightseer, as it contains an introductory chapter descriptive of the Albert Memorial inaugurated in Edinburgh by her Majesty, accompanied by an excellent photograph of the monument. Another feature is a descriptive photograph of the Livingstone Statue recently erected to the memory of the devoted missionary and explorer of Africa. This Guide to Edinburgh has been carefully compiled, and the plan adopted is that of dividing the city into three sections or walks, the starting-point of each being the Register House. The first walk is along Princes Street, with the picturesque houses of the Old Town and the Castle on the left, and the stately houses of the New Town on the right, with a noble valley between—the whole making a view unsurpassed for beauty and variety of feature. The row of monuments includes the Livingstone, Wilson, and Ramsay statues, and the noble Gothic structure erected to the memory of the Wizard of the North, under the basement arch of which he sits calmly looking on the city he loved so well. A distinguishing feature of this guide is the short yet accurate descriptions which it gives of the historic houses of the old town, now so rapidly lessening with the march of improvement. Cardinal Beaton's palace and the Mint have recently been removed to afford breathing room for the denizens of the Cowgate. Allan Ramsay's theatre has been razed to the ground, though the house in which he commenced business as a bookseller still stands in the High Street—a characteristic specimen of the old style of Scottish architecture. The houses associated with Burns are still mostly in existence, the only one destroyed being Clarinda's little dwelling in the Potterrow. Worshippers of the poet can still visit his haunts, such as Richmond's lodgings in Baxter's Close, the White Hart Inn in the Grassmarket, the Canongate Kilwinning Lodge in St. John Street, and the house of Lord Monboddo in the same street. Burns appears to have had a high opinion of this learned lawyer and daring speculator, whose daughter the poet describes in his address to Edinburgh:—

> "Fair Burnet, strikes the adoring eye,
> Heaven's beauties on my fancy shine;
> I see the Sire of Love on high,
> And own his work indeed divine."

At the end of the Guide are descriptions of a few places in the environs of Edinburgh which the tourist is recommended to visit, such as Roslin, Dalkeith, Lasswade, Dalmeny, and Aberdour. It should be mentioned that this Guide is beautifully printed, and illustrated with numerous woodcuts of the places of interest.

Edinburgh Daily Review, 10th April, 1877.

The unveiling of the Albert Equestrian Statue last August has suggested and given a name to this Guide. The handsome volume, illustrated by a photograph of the Livingstone Statue as well as of the Albert Memorial, may take its place at the head of all the Guides to our city. It is well-written, it is accurate, it shows culture in quoting Alexander Smith's description of the city, and it is illustrated by engravings which are themselves specimens of art. We know no better souvenir for visitors. In the next edition it would be well to show the extraordinary extension of Edinburgh to the west and south, which is still going on and gives no sign of being arrested even by the present Parliamentary boundary. The division of walks and routes adopted will be found useful by the stranger, who cannot do better than make the Register House his central point of departure.

THREE BEAUTIFUL TRIPS
TO THE
HIGHLANDS FROM EDINBURGH, AND BACK, IN ONE DAY.

Route No. 1.—To Loch Lomond, Loch Katrine, The Trossachs.

RAIL about 7 morning, from Waverley Station, by Stirling; arriving in Balloch about 9 o'clock. Steamer waiting for you, and starts immediately up Loch Lomond, arriving at Inversnaid about 11 o'clock. Coach across the hills to Loch Katrine (5 miles) in good time for the 1 o'clock boat, which occupies about an hour to sail down to the Trossachs, where a coach is waiting to drive you through the Trossachs Glen, also by the shores of Loch Achray, Loch Vennechar, arriving in Callander about 4 o'clock, in time for the train for Stirling, Glasgow, or Edinburgh.

PROBABLE COST OF THIS ROUTE.

	£ s d
3rd Class Fare from Edinburgh to Balloch,	0 4 0
1st Class Fare on Loch Lomond Boat,	0 2 6
Outside of Coach from Inversnaid,	0 2 6
Fare on Loch Katrine Boat,	0 2 6
Coach from Trossachs to Callander, 12 miles,	0 5 6
3rd Class Fare from Callander to Edinburgh,	0 4 4
	£1 1 4

Good Breakfast on Lochlomond boats, 2s. 6d.
The above route can be reversed.

Route No. 2.—To Loch Long, Arrochar, Tarbet, and Loch Lomond.

RAIL about 7 morning from the Caledonian Station, Princes Street, to Greenock, arriving about 9 o'clock, in time to catch the Loch Long boat for Arrochar, which it reaches about 11 o'clock. Coach in waiting for Tarbet, on Loch Lomond. (The distance is only 1½ miles, and is a beautiful walk; a smart walker will beat the coach.) At Tarbet you cross in the steamer to Inversnaid, on Loch Lomond, and return by Loch Katrine, the Trossachs, and Callander to Edinburgh; or you may take the steamer on Loch Lomond down to Balloch, and return by Dumbarton and Glasgow, and arrive in Edinburgh in the evening.

PROBABLE COST OF THIS ROUTE.

	£ s d
2nd Class Fare to Greenock,	£0 5 0
Loch Long Boat to Arrochar,	0 2 6
Coach to Tarbet,	0 2 6
	0 10 0
Steamer from Tarbet to Balloch,	0 2 0
1st Class Fare from do. to Glasgow,	0 2 3
2nd Class Fare to Edinburgh,	0 4 0
In all,	£0 18 3

If at Tarbet you return by Loch Katrine and the Trossachs the expense will be about 10s. extra.

Route No. 3.—To Loch Earn, Braes of Balquhidder, and Callander.

RAIL from Waverley Station, about 7 morning, for Crieff by Stirling, arriving about 10 o'clock. Four-horse coach waiting at the station during tourist season, for Comrie, St. Fillans, along the shores of Loch Earn to Lochearnhead. The scenery along this route is very beautiful, and in some places impressively grand. At Lochearnhead you get the train, which passes through some fine scenery,—such as Rob Roy's country, the Braes of Balquhidder, the shores of Loch Lubnaig, the Pass of Leny,—and arrive in Callander about 4 o'clock, from which Edinburgh can be reached the same evening.

If you wish to extend your journey for a day or so, Callander would be the right place to rest for the night, as in the morning you can get on to the Trossachs, Loch Katrine, Loch Awe, and on to Oban the same evening.

	£ s d
3rd Class Fare from Edinburgh to Crieff,	£0 5 2
Outside Coach Fare from Crieff to Lochearnhead, say 20 miles,	0 10 0
3rd Class Fare from Lochearnhead to Edinburgh,	0 5 6
	£1 0 8

TERMS AND HOURS OF ADMISSION TO PUBLIC BUILDINGS, AND OBJECTS OF INTEREST IN EDINBURGH AND ENVIRONS.

Fixed Fee or Gratuity.

Antiquarian Museum. Thursday and Friday, 10 till 4. 6d.
Aquarium, Waverley Market. Daily; in Summer, 6 to 10; Winter, 8 to 10. 6d.
Burns' Monument, Calton Hill. Daily, in Summer from 8 to 7; Winter, 10 to 3. 2d.
College Library, South Bridge. Daily, 10 till 4. 6d. for single individuals; 1s. for parties not exceeding 12. Strangers conducted by the Warder.
Hawthornden (by Rail, from Waverley Bridge Station), *entrance by Hawthornden Gate only*. Daily, 1s.
Holyrood Palace and Chapel Royal. Monday to Friday, from 11 till 6. 6d. (by ticket, got within the entrance on the left).
John Knox's House, High Street, Netherbow. Wednesday and Saturday, from 10 till 4. 6d.
Museum of Science and Art. Monday, Tuesday, and Thursday, from 10 till 4. 6d.
National Gallery of Paintings, Royal Institution. Thursday and Friday, from 10 till 4. 6d. Catalogues, 6d. Sticks and Umbrellas left at door, 1d.
Nelson's Monument, Calton Hill. Daily, 3d.
Rosslyn Chapel (by Rail, from Waverley Bridge Station, or by Coach, from 4 Princes Street). Daily, 1s. *Bona fide* parties of 10 and upwards, 6d. each.
Rosslyn Castle. Daily, 6d. Parties of 6, 3d. each.
Scott Monument (Top), Princes Street. Daily, 2d.
Statue Gallery, Royal Institution. Wednesday and Friday, from 10 till 4. 6d.

Free.

Advocates' Library, Parliament Square. Daily, 10 till 4. Saturdays, 10 till 1.
Antiquarian Museum, Royal Institution. Tuesday, Wednesday, and Saturday, from 10 till 4; and on Saturdays, from 7 till 9 evening.
Castle—Queen Mary's Apartment, &c. Daily.
Botanic Gardens, Inverleith Row. Monday to Friday, from 6 till 6; Saturdays, from 6 a.m. till 8 p.m. In Winter, from daylight till dusk.
The Lawson Seed Company's Nurseries, Inverleith Row. Daily (Sundays excepted), from 6 till 6. In Winter, from daylight till dusk.
Dalkeith Palace and Gardens. Wednesdays and Saturdays, during the absence of the family.
Donaldson's Hospital. Tuesday and Friday, from 2.30 till 4. By Order, which may be obtained from the Treasurer, J. Cook, Esq., W.S., 61 Castle Street; or from Stuart Neilson, Esq., W.S., 1 N. Charlotte St.
Heriot's Hospital, Lauriston. Admission daily, from 12 till 3, Saturdays and Sundays excepted. Orders obtained at the Treasurer's Chambers, 7 Royal Exchange, High Street.
Holyrood Palace and Chapel Royal. Saturdays, from 11 till 6.
Museum of Science and Art, Chambers Street. Wednesday, Friday, and Saturday, from 10 till 4; and on Friday and Saturday evenings, from 6 till 9.
National Gallery of Paintings, Royal Institution. Monday, Tuesday, Wednesday, and Saturday, from 10 till 5; also on Saturdays from 7 till 9 evening. Catalogues, 6d. Sticks and Umbrellas left at the door, 1d.
Parliament House, Parliament Square. Daily, 9 till 4, during the sitting of the Courts.
Phrenological Museum, Chambers Street. Saturdays, from 1 till 6; but strangers are admitted any day.
Regalia of Scotland, Castle. From 11 till 5 daily.
St Giles's Cathedral, High Street. Daily.
Statue Gallery, Royal Institution. Saturdays, 10 till 4.
Surgeons' Museum, Nicolson Street. Daily, *except Tuesday*, from 11 till 4.
Waverley Market. Daily, during Market hours; Summer, 7 to 10; Winter, 8 to 10. 1d.

New Winter Garden, West Coates, Haymarket, erected by Downie, Laird, & Laing, Nurserymen. Daily (*Sundays excepted*), till 6 p.m.

HOTELS, RESTAURANTS, AND DINING SALOONS.

For the excellence and extent of its Hotel accommodation, Edinburgh is unsurpassed by any city in the empire of equal population. Many of the buildings have been specially erected for the purpose, and some at a cost ranging from £14,000 to £25,000. They are, accordingly, generally well built, centrally situated, elegantly furnished, and amply provided with all the minor accessories of civilised life requisite to render them comfortable and attractive. The average rate of charges may be stated as follows:—For breakfast, 1s. to 3s.; for dinner, 1s. 9d. to 6s.; for tea, 1s. to 3s.; for bed, 1s. 6d. to 4s.; for private parlour, 2s. 6d. to 7s.; attendance extra. The following are a few of the more centrally situated:—

Family and General.

Royal (M'Gregor), 53 Princes Street.
The Palace, 109 Princes Street.
The Balmoral, 91 Princes Street.
Edinburgh (Middlemass), 36 Princes Street.
The Clarendon, 104 Princes Street.
Caledonian Hotel (Moore), 1 Castle Street.
*The Cockburn (Philip), 1 Cockburn Street.
Turkish Baths in connection with the above.
Waterloo, 24 Waterloo Place.
M'Kay's, 8 Princes Street.
Windsor Hotel, 100 Princes Street.
Kerr's, 133 George Street (*Private*).
*Regent (Darling), 20 Waterloo Place.
Royal British (Grieve), 22 Princes Street.
Bedford, 82 Princes Street.

Fairbairn's (*Private*), 127 George Street.
Roxburghe, 28 Charlotte Square.
Swain's, 5 Albyn Place.
London Hotel, St. Andrew Square.
Veitch's, 120 George Street.
Imperial, Market Street.
*The Waverley, 42 Princes Street and Waterloo Place.
Albert (Robertson), 25 Hanover Street.
*Crown (Miller), 2 West Register Street.
St. George's, 17 and 23 George Street.
Ship (M'Lean), 7 East Register Street.
Milne's, 24 Greenside Street.

Temperance Luncheon Rooms.

A. Ritchie & Son, 24 Princes Street.
Edinburgh Café Company, 70 Princes Street.

* *Temperance.*

James Middlemass & Co., 18 South Bridge, Edinburgh.

OUTFITS.

GENTLEMEN about to proceed ABROAD need not now experience the trouble of procuring the Articles of Outfit, and the information which they require, from Tradesmen in London, who may be unknown to them, or the too frequent annoyance, on arriving at their destination, of finding unnecessary Articles procured and essential ones omitted; but by proceeding to an Outfitter whose experience and standing are well known, and where they or their friends have the opportunity of examining the Articles *personally*, may at once be supplied with everything really necessary, without anything superfluous.

The Subscribers having for many years devoted their unremitting attention to this part of their Business, which has now become a regular and well-defined branch of trade, can appeal with confidence to the many families in Scotland whose sons or relatives they have had the honour of fitting out; and will have much pleasure in giving Gentlemen their assistance and advice, not only in the selection of Goods, but in their despatch of Shipment.

Missionaries and Teachers supplied on the most liberal terms.

PRINTED LISTS

with prices to all parts of the world, may be had on application, or will be sent free by post.

OUTFITS WASHED, MARKED, AND PACKED WHEN REQUESTED, AND FORWARDED TO ANY PORT IN THE UNITED KINGDOM.

CASH PRICES, AND NO DISCOUNT.

JAMES MIDDLEMASS & CO.,

Clothiers, Shirtmakers, and General Outfitters,

18 SOUTH BRIDGE, EDINBURGH.

18 SOUTH BRIDGE, EDINBURGH, FIVE MINUTES

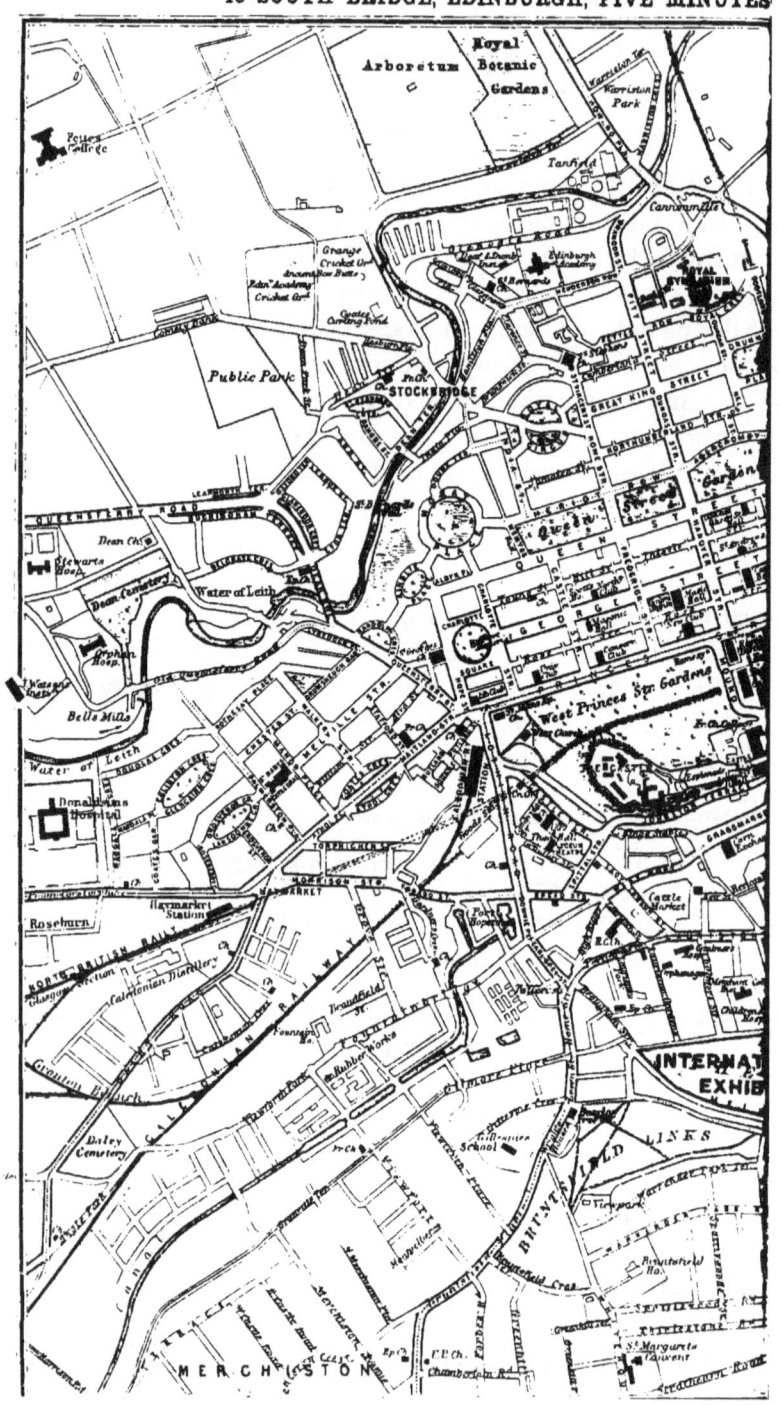

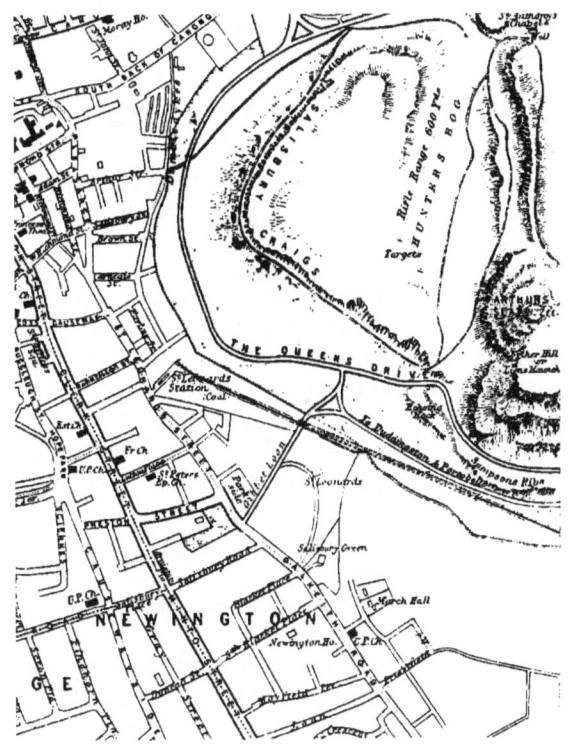

James Middlemass & Co., 18 South Bridge, Edinburgh.

LETTER from CHARLES H. MEIN, Esq., Bombay Bank.

15 CUMIN PLACE, GRANGE,
EDINBURGH, 6*th January*, 1872.

Messrs. JAS. MIDDLEMASS & COMPY.,
18 South Bridge, Edinburgh.

GENTLEMEN,—In answer to your inquiry, I have much pleasure in stating that my entire Outfit for Bombay, which I entrusted to your care, has come to hand in perfect order.

I am also happy to inform you that everything connected with it gives me great satisfaction, and that I consider the style and workmanship of the various articles, and the suitability of the materials, to be unexceptionable, while the prices, considering the excellent quality of the goods, are very moderate.

Your large experience in the Outfitting trade has saved me much worry and trouble in getting up my Outfit, as well as from the unnecessary expense of purchasing anything that is not actually required.

I have also to thank you for your attention and promptitude in getting everything ready for me, and to request that you will preserve all my measures, that I may, from time to time, get from you what articles I may in future require.—I am, Gentlemen, yours truly,

CHAS. H. MEIN.

Of the Bombay Bank.

LETTER from the Rev. GEORGE MACALLISTER, Nusseerabad.

NUSSEERABAD, RAJPOOTANA, INDIA,
17*th April*, 1872.

BEFORE leaving for India last year, Mr. Middlemass, South Bridge, furnished me with an Outfit, which, I am happy to say, has been thoroughly satisfactory in every respect. The materials have been of the best quality, neatly fitted, and have worn well.

I have much pleasure in recording the valuable assistance which I received from the Firm in considering what the Outfit should consist of. Valuable suggestions were made to me, which I acted upon, and am now reaping the advantage of them.

From their experience of what is required, many little things were provided which I would never have thought of, but which have since saved me from a world of trouble.

GEO. MACALLISTER, M.A.

EDINBURGH CASTLE FROM THE SOUTH ABOUT 1640

CONTENTS

	Page		Page		Page
Abbey Sanctuary	39	Cemeteries—		Colinton	63
Adam Square	52	Calton	46	College Wynd	54
Advocate's Close	32	Canongate	38	Corstorphine	64
Advocate's Library	30	Dean	49	County Hall, The	26
Advocates, The Faculty of	30	Grange	58	Covenant Close	33
Alison Square	55	Greyfriars'	24	Cowgate	52
Allan Ramsay's House	21	Warriston	50		
Allan Ramsay's Shop	28			Craigmillar Castle	61
Anchor Close	33	Churches and Chapels—		Crown Room	20
Ancient City Cross	32	Barclay	57		
Art, Works of. *See* Monuments and Statues.		Broughton Place U.P.	50	Dalhousie Castle	61
Assembly Close	33	Buccleuch	54	Dalkeith	61
Assembly Rooms, The	48	Buccleuch Free	54	Dalmeny	65
		Canongate	38		
Banks—		Chalmers's Memorial	58	Darien House	55
Bank of Scotland	23	Gaelic, Free	17	Deaf and Dumb Institution	51
British Linen Company	47	Greyfriars', Old	23	Dean Bridge	48
Clydesdale	48	Greyfriars', New	23	Dickson's Close	34
Commercial	48	Infirmary Street U.P.	52	Dining Saloons	8
National	47	Lady Yester's	52		
Royal	47	Lauriston Place U.P.	57	Dirleton	66
Union	29	Magdalen	23		
		New North, Free	56	Duddingston	61
Bass Rock	66	Nicolson Street U.P.	54		
		Queen Margaret's	19	Edinburgh Academy	51
Baxter's Close	23	Sacred Heart	56	Elphinstone's Court	35
Bishop's Close	34	St Andrew's	47	Ferguson's Tomb	38
Blackfriars' Street	34	St Augustine	23	Fleshmarket Close	33
Blair's Close	21	St Columba's	17	Fountain, The Abbey	39
Blind Asylum	54	St Cuthbert's	16	Free Church Assembly Hall, The	22
Botanic Gardens	50	St George's	48	Free Church College, The	51
Bristo Port	56	St George's Episcopal	50		
Bruntsfield Links	57	St George's Free	48	General's Entry	55
Buccleuch Place	55	St Giles's	27	George IV. Bridge	23
Byre's Close	31	St John's Episcopal	16	George Square	55
		St John's Free	22	George Street	47
Burntisland and Aberdour	65	St Luke's Free	49	Grange House	58
		St Mark's	17		
Cab Fares	69	St Mary's	50	Granton	60
		St Mary's Free	50		
Calton Hill, The	46	St Mary's Roman Catholic	50	Grassmarket, The	26
Canongate, The	36	St Paul's Episcopal	50		
Canongate Tolbooth	38	St Stephen's	51	Hawthornden	62
Canonmills	50	St Thomas's Episcopal	48		
Carrubbers' Close	33	Trinity Episcopal	49	High School	44
Castle, The	18	Tron	33	High Street	31
Chalmers's Close	34	West Coates	48	Holyrood Palace and Chapel	40
Charles Street	55	Colinton	65	Horse Wynd	54

CONTENTS.

	Page
HOSPITALS—	
Donaldson's	48
Gillespie's	57
Fettes	49
Heriot's	56
Merchant Maidens'	57
Stewart's	49
Trades' Maidens'	58
Watson's, George	56
Watson's, John	49
Hotels, &c.	8
Hunter Square	33
Hyndford's Close	35
Infirmary Street	52
INVERESK	61
James's Court	22
John Knox's Grave	29
John Knox's House	35
KIRKLISTON	65
JUNIPER GREEN	64
Lady Stair's Close	23
LASSWADE, Walk from ROSSLYN to	63
LEITH	59
Leith Walk	50
Leith Wynd	36
LIBRARIES—	
Advocates'	30
Signet	31
University	53
Market Cross	32
Meadows	58
Merchiston Castle	57
Middleton's Entry	55
Milne's Court	22
Milne Square	33
Milton House	38
Mint Court	35
MONUMENTS—	
Burns's (by Hamilton)	44
Catherine Sinclair's	49
Martyrs'	46
Melville's	47
National	46
Nelson's	46
Playfair's	46
Scott's (by Kemp)	14
Smith's, Alexander (by Brodie and Drummond)	50
Stewart's	46
78th Reg. Memorial Cross	18
Moray House	37
Morningside	57
Morocco Land	36

	Page
MUSEUMS—	
Antiquarian	15
Phrenological	53
Royal College of Surgeons	54
Science and Art	53
University	53
Music Hall, The	48
MUSSELBURGH	60
National Gallery, The	15
Nether Bow, The	35
NEWBATTLE ABBEY	61
NEWHAVEN	59
New Street	36
Nicolson Street and Square	54
NORTH BERWICK	66
North Bridge	52
Observatory, New Royal	46
Observatory, Old	46
Old Fishmarket Close	33
Omnibuses (Town and Country)	8
Paisley's Close	34
Panmure Close	38
Parliament House, The	29
Parliament Square	29
Pentland Hills	64
Philosophical Institution	50
Physician's Hall	49
Playhouse Close	36
Police Office	32
Porteous Mob, Account of	27
PORTOBELLO	60
Post Office, General	46
Potterrow	55
Princes Street	14
Princes Street Gardens, East	14
Princes Street Gardens, West	14
Prisons, The	45
Protestant Institute of Scotland	23
Queensberry House	38
QUEENSFERRY, SOUTH	64
Queen Mary's Apartments	41
Queen Mary's Room (Castle)	20
Queen's Park, The	43
Queen Street	49
Register House	13
Reservoir, The	21
Richmond Street (East and West)	54
Riddle's Close	23
ROSSLYN	62
ROSSLYN CASTLE	63
Royal College of Surgeons	54
Royal Exchange, The	32

	Page
Royal Infirmary	52
Royal Institution, The	15
St Andrew Square	46
St Bernard's Well	49
St John Street	36
St Margaret's Convent	57
St Mary's Street	36
Sculpture Gallery, The	15
Sempill's Close	22
Sheriff Court Buildings	23
Signet Library	31
Sinclair Fountain, The	16
South Bridge	52
South Gray's Close	34
Stamp Office Close	33
STATUES—	
Blair, Lord President (by Chantrey)	30
Boyle, Lord President (Steell)	30
Burns (Flaxman)	16
Cockburn, Lord (Brodie)	30
Charles II. (Foreign Artist)	29
Forbes of Culloden (Roubiliac)	30
Dundas of Arniston (Chantrey)	30
George IV. (Chantrey)	48
Hopetoun, Earl of	47
Jeffrey, Lord (Steell)	30
Melville, Viscount, First (Chantrey)	30
Melville, Viscount, Second (Steell)	48
Pitt (Chantrey)	48
Queen, The (Steell)	15
Ramsay, Allan (Steell)	16
Scott, Sir Walter (Steell)	14
Watt, James	52
Wellington (Steell)	13
Wilson, John (Steell)	14
York, Duke of (Campbell)	16
Steamers from Granton and Leith	68
Strichen's Close	34
Tanfield Hall	50
TANTALLON CASTLE	66
Theatre Royal	50
Toddrick's Wynd	34
Tolbooth, The Old	26
TRINITY	69
Tweeddale Court	35
United Presb. Church Synod Hall	50
University, The	53
Victoria or Assembly Hall	22
Waterloo Place	46
West Bow, The	22
Whiteford House	34
Whitehorse Close	39
York Place	50

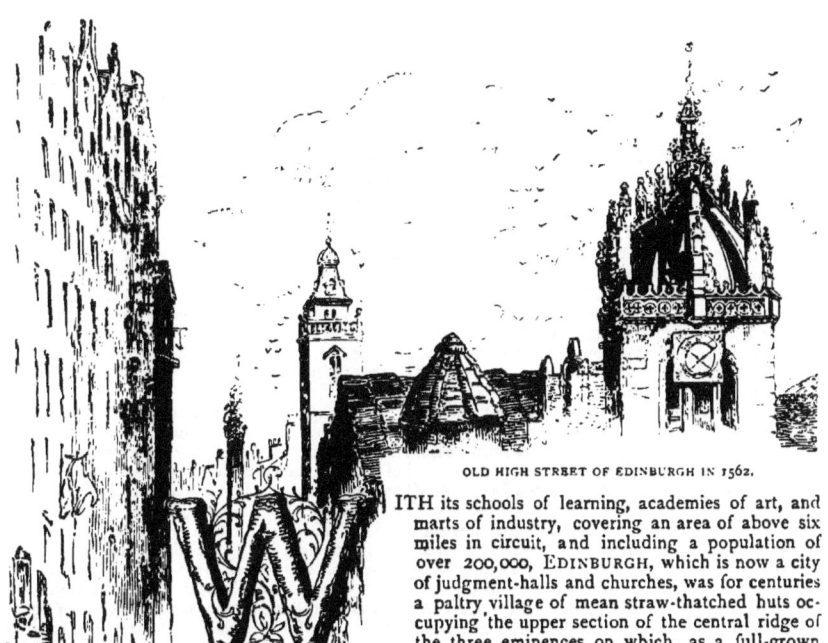

OLD HIGH STREET OF EDINBURGH IN 1562.

WITH its schools of learning, academies of art, and marts of industry, covering an area of above six miles in circuit, and including a population of over 200,000, EDINBURGH, which is now a city of judgment-halls and churches, was for centuries a paltry village of mean straw-thatched huts occupying the upper section of the central ridge of the three eminences on which, as a full-grown city, it is now situated, and was surrounded on all sides by a dense natural forest, interspersed with heaths and marshes, infested by the elk, the wild boar, and the wolf. It is unquestionably daughter of the magnificent fortress of rock which, seven acres in area a-top, rises sheer, often to a height of 250 feet, above the adjoining valleys, and the use of which as a military stronghold dates from the early days of the Saxon heptarchy.

When the city first burst the confines of the area of the Castle rock, and began to extend along the ridge declining eastward, history does not inform us; but it already figures as a considerable village so early as 854, and from the year 1020 it ceases, with the adjacent territory, to belong to Northumbria, becoming henceforth subject *de jure*, if not always *de facto*, to the kings of Scotland. The village, which the city then was, was first raised to the rank of a burgh in 1129, by David I., who held his court in the Castle; and it was he who founded the Abbey of Holyrood, and granted, by charter, to its canons the power to erect the burgh of Canongate, between the "church and the town." William the Lion, the second in succession to David, first gave to the city the dignity of a royal burgh, assembled within it the estates of the realm, and converted it into a place of mintage for the king's currency; and Alexander III. made it the depository of the insignia of royalty and the records of the kingdom.

In 1327-28, Robert the Bruce held a convention of estates in the Abbey of Holyrood, in which representatives of the city, as a burgh, sat and deliberated; and in such honour was the city held by this prince, that we find him, in the following year, conferring upon the corporation lordship over "the harbour and mills of Leith, with their appurtenances, for payment of 22 merks yearly." So small and mean, however, was this now proud city, that up to this period and later, it would appear, the population did not amount to more than 2000, housed in mere thatch-roofed fabrics, 400 in number, none of them being above 20 feet in elevation; and so stinted was the accommodation, that Froissart, who visited it in 1384, found within it no available lodging worthy of the knights that accompanied him, who were in consequence compelled to take up their quarters in the castle of Dalkeith.

About 1438, the city became the favourite residence of the kings of the Stuart family; and James III., by special proclamation, constituted the provost hereditary sheriff within the burgh, raised to the rank of a county, and vested the Town Council with legislative powers within the same limits.

In the days of Mary of Guise, and her better known but ill-starred daughter, the ancient royalty began to assume the shape in which, in the main, we still find it—as a dense array of tall stone fabrics extending, inclusive of the Canongate, a mile in length from the Castle to the palace of Holyrood, with as many as one hundred closes—themselves miniature streets—sometimes not more than four or five feet wide, branching away at right angles to the main street down to the valleys running parallel with the line of the city on the north and south.

Within these limits the city continued to confine itself all through the reigns of James VI. and the Charleses. Thus, for two or three hundred years after it became the acknowledged capital of the kingdom, were the citizens content with the ancient barriers: and yet the appearance presented, with its tall piles, three main spires, grand castle rock, and the striking contour of its situation and environment, was a singularly imposing one. Such was the city as it seemed to My Lord Protector when he was honourably escorted into Edinburgh, on the 4th of October 1648; such it was as known *in transitu* twice over to humanely-devout, rough, old Samuel Johnson, and, nearly through life, to his contemporary, the clear-minded David Hume; and so, too, it looked to Oliver Goldsmith when attending classes in the University; to Robert Burns, also, and the young eyes of Walter Scott.

In its antique form, the city was a focus of memories, dear to all Scotchmen, and it was nothing wonderful that patriotic citizens, in whose eyes the integrity of the civic life was deemed as sacred as that of the individual, should have hesitated to accept innovations sure to rupture old ties, dissolve the most hallowed associations, and revolutionise the manners of the whole community. Accordingly, when Provost Drummond, after a world of effort, succeeded with the public, and proceeded, 21st October 1763, to lay the foundation stone of the North Bridge, it was rather by representing to them the excellent roadway it would open up to Leith than as a means of extension to the city, that he gained his point and obtained the sanction of his fellow-citizens. But it was not till 1767 that an Act of Parliament was obtained for extending the royalty, "over the fields to northward;" and it was 1772 before, at a cost of £18,000, the structure was finished as a public highway. During the nine years which elapsed between the foundation and the completion, a number of citizens, dissatisfied with the delay, began to build a new town on the south, partly within and partly beyond the confines of the royalty. Thus originated Brown Square, Argyle Square, Adam Square, and George Square, with the streets adjoining.

In the year 1785, a breach was made on the south side of the High Street, and a bridge-way of twenty-two arches founded, continuing the road along the North Bridge straight south over the Cowgate; and this street, which was called the South Bridge, of which all the arches are now hidden save one, soon became, what it still is, one of the most active business quarters of the city; and immediately on its completion in 1789 the foundations were laid, at its southern extremity, of the massive structure appropriated to the use of our ancient and world-famous University.

And now, at length, with these, and other more recent extensions, a city is realised, which, for grandly-picturesque beauty, interesting associations, and nobly-romantic situation, has hardly a rival among the cities of either ancient or modern times. Approached from any quarter, it never fails to strike a stranger with impressions of a character altogether novel; while the heights within and around, as well as the streets and valleys, by night as by day, present aspects which startle, now by their beauty, now by their still sublimity, and now by their rich variety and range of scene. From the Calton Hill alone—conspicuous for its monuments, and half encircled midway up by a range of almost princely residences—which rises 344 feet, at the eastern extremity of the northern eminence, a view is obtained of the city, with its surrounding heights and gardened suburbs, the island-gemmed Forth in the far distance, and the outflanking Grampians to northward, that even Naples cannot match.

Edinburgh is less a place of manufacturing activity than the majority of modern cities; and the impression of repose it creates suggests ideas of culture, rather than of rough-visaged, rough-handed industrial life. Accordingly, what with its schools of art and seminaries of learning, at the top of which ranks the University—which, for its medical faculty especially, is of more than European fame—and what with the cultivated society, with its appliances, which these involve and attract, there are few cities which offer equal advantages for stimulating the intellect, educating the taste, and enlarging the heart. Its Schools, with their long line of distinguished teachers, are of world-wide celebrity; and from them, as from the city itself, have proceeded some of the greatest men the country has produced. And in proof of this we have but to cite the long list of distinguished men who have been educated at the High School and the Edinburgh Academy. It is from Edinburgh, also, others being judges, that the most prominent intellectual movements of the present age have emanated, and the greatest and wisest thinker now living was educated at its University, and began his literary career half a century ago within its walls. It is the city of David Hume, of Sir Walter Scott, and, in a sense, of Thomas Carlyle; and these three men nearly sum up the whole intellectual tendency of the present time.

The romantic beauty of site and rich historic associations of Edinburgh have been described by many able pens. From the days of Defoe and Smollett to those of Scott, Chambers, and Cockburn, volumes innumerable have been published on this theme, all of them interesting, and many of them destined to live with the language in which they are written. But there is no description of the city that we know of that can at all compare, in felicity of language and fulness of detail, with one by the late Alexander Smith, which occurs in a delightful volume of Home Travel, entitled "A Summer in Skye," issued by the eminent London publishing house of Messrs A. Strahan & Co., and from which, by their kindness and courtesy, we are permitted to make an extract or two. Like all the prose that proceeded from the writer's pen, these extracts bear the unmistakeable stamp of a rich poetic faculty combined with rare descriptive powers, and may be termed—

PICTURES OF EDINBURGH BY A POET.

Romantic Beauty of the New Town.

"Every true Scotsman believes Edinburgh to be the most picturesque city in the world; and truly, standing on the Calton Hill at early morning, when the smoke of fires newly-kindled hangs in azure swathes and veils about the Old Town —which from that point resembles a huge lizard, the Castle its head, church-spires spikes upon its scaly back, creeping up from its lair beneath the Crags to look out on the morning world—one is quite inclined to pardon the enthusiasm of the North Briton. The finest view from the interior is obtained from the corner of St Andrew Street, looking west. Straight before you the Mound crosses the valley, bearing the white Academy buildings; beyond, the Castle lifts, from grassy slopes and billows of summer foliage, its weather-stained towers and fortifications, the Half-Moon battery giving the folds of its standard to the wind. Living in Edinburgh there abides, above all things, a sense of its beauty. Hill, crag, castle, rock, blue stretch of sea, the picturesque ridge of the Old Town, the squares and terraces of the New—these things seen once are not to be forgotten. The quick life of to-day sounding around the relics of antiquity, and overshadowed by the august traditions of a kingdom, makes residence in Edinburgh more impressive than residence in any other British city. What a poem is that Princes Street! The puppets of the busy, many-coloured hour move about on its pavement, while across the ravine Time has piled up the Old Town, ridge on ridge, gray as a rocky coast washed and worn by the foam of centuries; peaked and jagged by gable and roof; windowed from basement to cope; the whole surmounted by St Giles's airy crown. The New is there looking at the Old. Two Times are brought face to face, and are yet separated by a thousand years. Wonderful on winter nights, when the gully is filled with darkness, and out of it rises, against the sombre blue and the frosty stars, that mass and bulwark of gloom, pierced and quivering with innumerable lights. There is nothing in Europe to match that, I think. Could you but roll a river down the valley it would be sublime. Finer still, to place one's-self near the Burns Monument and look toward the Castle. It is more astonishing than an Eastern dream. A city rises up before you painted by fire on night. High in air a bridge of lights leaps the chasm; a few emerald lamps, like glow-worms, are moving silently about in the railway station below; a solitary crimson one is at rest. That ridged and chimneyed bulk of blackness, with splendour bursting out at every pore, is the wonderful Old Town, where Scottish history mainly transacted itself; while, opposite, the modern Princes Street is blazing throughout its length. During the day the Castle looks down upon the city as if out of another world; stern with all its peacefulness, its garniture of trees, its slopes of grass. The rock is dingy enough in colour, but after a shower its lichens laugh out greenly in the returning sun, while the rainbow is brightening on the lowering sky beyond. How deep the shadow which the Castle throws at noon over the gardens at its feet where the children play! How grand when giant bulk and towery crown blacken against sunset! Fair, too, the New Town sloping to the sea. From George Street, which crowns the ridge, the eye is led down sweeping streets of stately architecture to the villas and woods that fill the lower ground, and fringe the shore; to the bright azure belt of the Forth with its smoking steamer or its creeping sail; beyond, to the shores of Fife, soft blue, and flecked with fleeting shadows in the keen, clear light of spring, dark purple in the summer heat, tarnished gold in the autumn haze; and farther away still, just distinguishable on the paler sky, the crest of some distant peak, carrying the imagination into the illimitable world. Residence in Edinburgh is an education in itself. Its beauty refines one, like being in love. It is perennial, like a play of Shakspere's. 'Nothing can stale its infinite variety.'"

Picturesque Beauty of the Old Town.

"From a historical and picturesque point of view, the Old Town is the most interesting part of Edinburgh; and the great street running from Holyrood to the Castle—in various portions of its length called the Lawnmarket, the High Street, and the Canongate—is the most interesting part of the Old Town. In that street the houses preserve their ancient appearance; they climb up heavenward, story upon story, with outside stairs and wooden panellings, all strangely peaked and gabled. With the exception of the inhabitants, who exist amidst squalor, and filth, and evil smells undeniably modern, everything in this long street breathes of the antique world. If you penetrate the narrow wynds that run at right angles from it, you see traces of ancient gardens. Occasionally the original names are retained, and they touch the visitor pathetically, like the scent of long-withered flowers. Old armorial bearings may yet be traced above the doorways. Two centuries ago fair eyes looked down from yonder window. If we but knew it, every crazy tenement has its tragic story; every crumbling wall could its tale unfold. The Canongate is Scottish history fossilised. What ghosts of kings and queens walk there! What strifes of steel-clad nobles! What wretches borne along, in the sight of peopled windows, to the grim embrace of the 'Maiden!' What hurrying of burgesses to man the city walls at the approach of the Southron! What lamentations over disastrous battle days! James rode up this street on his way to Flodden. Montrose was dragged up hither on a hurdle, and smote, with disdainful glance, his foes gathered together on the balcony. Jenny Geddes flung her stool at the priest in the church yonder. John Knox came up here to his house after his interview with Mary at Holyrood—grim and stern, and unmelted by the tears of the queen. The Pretender rode down here, his eyes dazzled by the glitter of his father's crown, while bagpipes skirled around, and Jacobite ladies, with white knots in their bosoms, looked down from lofty windows, admiring the beauty of the 'Young Ascanius,' and his long yellow hair. David Hume had his dwelling in this street, and trod its pavements, much meditating the wars of the Roses and the Parliament, and the fates of English sovereigns. One day a burly ploughman from Ayrshire, with swarthy features and wonderful black eyes, came down here and turned into yonder churchyard to stand, with cloudy lids and forehead reverently bared, beside the grave of poor Fergusson. Down this street, too, often limped a little boy, Walter Scott by name, destined in after years to write its 'Chronicles.' The Canongate once seen is never to be forgotten. The visitor starts a ghost at every step. Nobles, grave senators, jovial lawyers, had once their abodes here. In the old, low-roofed rooms, halfway to the stars, philosophers talked, wits coruscated, and gallant young fellows, sowing wild oats in the middle of last century, wore rapiers and lace ruffles, and drank claret jovially out of silver stoups. In every room a minuet has been walked, while chairmen and linkmen clustered on the pavement beneath."

Intellectual Supremacy of Edinburgh.

"With Castle, tower, church-spire, and pyramid rising into sunlight out of garden spaces and belts of foliage, and throned on crags, Edinburgh takes every eye; and, not content with supremacy in beauty, she claims an intellectual supremacy also. She is a patrician amongst British cities, 'A penniless lass wi' a lang pedigree.' She has wit if she lacks wealth: she counts great men against millionaires. The success of the actor is insecure until thereunto Edinburgh has set her seal. The poet trembles before the Edinburgh critics. The singer respects the delicacy of the Edinburgh ear. Coarse London may roar with applause; fastidious Edinburgh sniffs disdain, and sneers reputations away. London is the stomach of the empire—Edinburgh the quick, subtle, far-darting brain." . . . . "Edinburgh is not only in point of beauty the first of British cities—but, considering its population, the general tone of its society is more intellectual than that of any other. In no other city will you find so general an appreciation of books, art, music, and objects of antiquarian interest. It is peculiarly free from the taint of the ledger and the counting-house. It is a Weimar without a Goethe—Boston without its nasal twang."

Edinburgh the first City in the Empire for a Literary or Retired Life.

"Of all British cities, Edinburgh—Weimar-like in its intellectual and æsthetic leanings, Florence-like in its freedom from the stains of trade, and more than Florence-like in its beauty—is the one best suited for the conduct of a lettered life. The city as an entity does not stimulate like London, the present moment is not nearly so intense, life does not roar and chafe—it murmurs only; and this interest of the hour, mingled with something of the quietude of distance and the past—which is the spiritual atmosphere of the city—is the most favourable of all conditions for intellectual work or intellectual enjoyment. You have libraries — you have the society of cultivated men and women—you have the eye constantly fed by beauty—the Old Town, jagged, picturesque, piled up; and the airy, open, coldly-sunny, unhurried, uncrowded streets of the New Town—and, above all, you can 'sport your oak,' as they say at Cambridge, and be quit of the world, the gossip, and the dun. In Edinburgh, you do not require to create quiet for yourself; you can have it readymade. Life is leisurely; but it is not the leisure of a village, arising from a deficiency of ideas and motives—it is the leisure of a city reposing grandly on tradition and history, which has done its work, which does not require to weave its own clothing, to dig its own coals, to smelt its own iron. And then, in Edinburgh, above all British cities, you are released from the vulgarising dominion of the hour. The past confronts you at every street corner. The Castle looks down out of history on its gayest thoroughfare. The winds of fable are blowing across Arthur's Seat. Old kings dwelt in Holyrood. Go out of the city where you will, the past attends you like a cicerone. Go down to North Berwick, and the red shell of Tantallon speaks to you of the might of the Douglases. Across the sea, from the gray-green Bass, through a cloud of gannets, comes the sigh of prisoners. From the long sea-board of Fife—which you can see from George Street — starts a remembrance of the Jameses. Queen Mary is at Craigmillar, Napier at Merchiston, Ben Jonson and Drummond at Hawthornden, Prince Charles in the little inn at Duddingston; and if you go out to Linlithgow, there is the smoke of Bothwellhaugh's fusee, and the Great Regent falling in the crooked street. Thus the past checkmates the present."

VIEW FROM THE TERRACE OF THE SCOTT MONUMENT.

"WHAT a poem is that Princes Street! The puppets of the busy, many-coloured hour move about on its pavement, while across the ravine Time has piled up the Old Town, ridge on ridge, gray as a rocky coast washed and worn by the foam of centuries; peaked and jagged by gable and roof; windowed from basement to cope; the whole surmounted by St. Giles's airy crown. The New is there looking at the Old. Two Times are brought face to face, and are yet separated by a thousand years. The Castle, too, looks down upon the city as if out of another world; stern with all its peacefulness, its garniture of trees, its slopes of grass. How deep the shadow which it throws at noon over the gardens at its feet where the children play! How grand when giant bulk and towery crown blacken against sunset!"— *Alexander Smith.*

"Even thus, methinks, a city reared should be—
  Yes, an imperial city, that might hold
Five times a hundred noble towns in fee;
  And either with the might of Babel old,
Or the rich Roman pomp of empery,
  Might stand compare—highest in arts enrolled,
Highest in arms, brave tenement for the free!

Thus should her towers be raised, with vicinage
  Of clear bold hills, that curve her very streets,
As if to vindicate, 'mid choicest seats
  Of Art, abiding Nature's majesty!"—*Hallam.*

EAST FRONT OF EDINBURGH CASTLE ABOUT 1750.

IN proceeding to describe the various public buildings and places of interest, we shall divide the city into Three Sections or Walks—a central, northern, and southern ; and shall take as the starting and terminating point of each a building pretty generally known—the GENERAL REGISTER HOUSE. Any particular street or building, however, may be readily found by glancing, in the one case at the headline of the page, and in the other at the prominent black titling lines in the body of the page itself. The list of streets at the head of each section or walk will show the general outline of each.

I.

The General Register House—Princes Street—Lothian Road (a portion of)—Castle Terrace—Back of Castle—Castle—Castle Hill—Lawnmarket—Bank Street—George IV. Bridge—Candlemaker Row—West Port—Grassmarket—West Bow—High Street—Canongate—Holyrood—Queen's Park and Drive—Arthur's Seat—Abbey Hill—Regent Road—Calton Hill—Waterloo Place—Register House.

The Old Register House.—This noble edifice, for the preservation of the public and legal records of the kingdom, was begun in 1772, but was not fully completed till 1822. The entire cost is said to have been somewhere about £80,000. Built in the Italian style, from a design by Mr Robert Adam, it is in the form of a square, with a large central dome, 50 feet in diameter and 80 feet in height, and two small turrets at each corner. Viewed from the front, which is protected by an elegant stone screen wall, the building is 200 feet in length and 120 in breadth, and contains over 100 apartments for the transaction of public business. In the numerous fire-proof chambers of the interior are deposited a vast quantity of valuable and curious historical and legal documents—such as the letter of the Scottish barons to the Pope in 1320, the acts of settlement of the Scottish crown upon the Stuarts in 1371 and 1373, the records of the National Parliaments, of the Privy Council, and of the Exchequer, the deed of institution given by James V. under which the Court of Session now sits, the Treaty of Union, &c., and copies or transcripts of all the title-deeds of property, legal contracts, mortgages, suits at law, &c., from a very early period.

The Wellington Statue.—In front stands a handsome equestrian statue in bronze, by John

Steell, R.S.A., of the Duke of Wellington, which was first unveiled to public view on the 18th of

June 1852, and cost £10,000. The pedestal, which is composed of Peterhead syenite, is 13 feet high; while the statue itself, which represents the Duke in an attitude of command on a rearing charger, is nearly 14 feet high.—A little to the west, behind the present building, and entering from West Register Street, stands

The New Register House.—Designed by Mr. Robert Matheson, of Her Majesty's Board of Works, this handsome building, which is also in the Italian style, was completed in 1860 at a cost of nearly £27,000. It was intended chiefly for the preservation of the registers of births, deaths, and marriages in Scotland, but is also used for other purposes connected with the courts of law.

A few paces farther west, in the same street, is **Venetian Buildings,** perhaps the handsomest business premises in the city, and the extensive town establishment of Messrs Cowan & Co., papermakers. Built in 1865, from a design by Messrs. George Beattie & Son, architects, this structure is a gorgeous specimen of what is termed the pure Venetian Gothic, the highest development of which is only to be seen in the magnificent palatial residences of the Venetian nobility, so glowingly described by Ruskin. The total cost of the building alone is understood to have been about £7000; and although somewhat hidden from public view, it is really a splendid addition to our street architecture.—Returning eastwards, and descending, we enter

PRINCES STREET,

the principal street and fashionable promenade of the New Town. One hundred feet wide, and a mile in length, with a fine southern exposure, and noble pleasure-grounds extending nearly the whole length of the street, and the bold rugged outline of the Old Town crowning, with spire, and tower, and turret, the opposite height, "and all the steep slope down," and the Castle on its rocky throne, towering, queen-like, in high state, above all, it forms one of the finest streets and most beautiful promenades to be found in any city in Europe. It contains most of the best-stocked, highest-rented, and handsomest business premises and shops in the city, and is the street *par excellence* of hotels, there being no fewer than twelve of these in it of various classes. The value of the stock in some of the higher class shops will run from £5000 to £20,000, and their rents from £250 to £1000.—A few paces along, on the other side, within the railings, is

The Waverley Fruit and Flower Market.—This handsome structure, erected by the Corporation in 1876, at a cost of £25,000, forms a graceful finish to this noble street. It is built wholly of iron. The upper floor is laid out in walks and garden plots, while below are galleries for promenading, and on the ground floor, shops for the sale of fruits and flowers, and an Aquarium. On the opposite side of the Waverley Bridge, within the Princes Street Gardens, there is a bronze statue to the memory of Dr. Livingstone, the great missionary traveller, sculptured by Mrs. D. O. Hill.—Continuing our walk westwards, we reach the most beautiful work of art in Edinburgh.

The Scott Monument.—This elegant structure was erected in 1840-44, in honour of the author of the Waverley Novels, and cost upwards of £15,000. It is in the form of an open crucial Gothic spire, supported on four grand Early English arches, which serve as a canopy to the statue, and is about 200 feet high. A staircase in the interior of one of the columns leads to a series of galleries, to which visitors are admitted on payment of twopence. Under the central basement arch is a marble statue, by Steell, of Sir Walter, with a figure of his favourite dog, Maida, at his feet; it was inaugurated in 1846,

and cost £2000. In the niches above the several arches are figures of some of the leading characters in his works. The architect was a self-taught genius named George Meikle Kemp, the son of a shepherd at Newhall, on the southern slope of the Pentland Hills, near Edinburgh, who was accidentally drowned in the Union Canal before the work was completed. Immediately to the west is a bronze statue, the work of Mr. Hutcheson, R.S.A., erected to the memory of Adam Black, Lord Provost and M.P. for the city, and publisher of the *Encyclopædia Britannica;* opposite which is the magnificent building, **The Royal Hotel** (Macgregor), having accommodation for upwards of 300 guests.

East Princes Street Gardens.—The low-lying portion of these grounds, through which the railway now passes, used to be covered with water, called the Nor' Loch.

Professor Wilson's Statue in bronze, by Steell, occupies a prominent position to the west of the Scott Monument; of colossal dimensions, it gives a good idea of what Christopher North, a veritable "lion-like man," was in the days of his flesh.—A few steps bring us to

The Royal Institution, an important Grecian-looking building. This structure was founded on piles in 1823, and finished a few years afterwards at a cost of £40,000. It was designed by the late W. H. Playfair, and is in the pure Doric style of architecture, of the era of Pericles. Colonnades extend along its sides, columned porticoes adorn its north and south ends, and sphinxes surmount its angles; over the principal entrance is a colossal sitting statue of the Queen in her robes of state, sculptured by Steell. In the interior are the apartments of the Board of Trustees for Manufactures in Scotland, and those of the Royal Society, a Gallery of Sculpture, and the Antiquarian Museum.

THE ROYAL INSTITUTION.

The Sculpture Gallery, admission to which is obtained on Wednesdays and Fridays from 12 till 4, for 6d., and on Saturdays from 10 till 4, *free*, contains casts of the Elgin marbles, of all the celebrated statues of antiquity, of the well-known Ghiberti gates of Florence, and a valuable series of casts of antique Greek and Roman busts, a collection originally made at Rome by the Alborini family, from whom they were purchased for the Gallery.

The Antiquarian Museum is open on Thursdays and Fridays from 10 till 4, when a charge of 6d. is made for admission—on Tuesdays, Wednesdays, and Saturdays, visitors are admitted *free*. Among the multifarious contents of the Museum may be noticed an interesting collection of Egyptian antiquities; sculptures, terra-cottas, &c., from various countries; ancient British implements, warlike and domestic; specimens of Romano-British pottery and glass manufacture; old Scotch wood-carvings; various instruments of punishment and torture used in Scotland; the Maiden, or Scottish guillotine, by which the Regent Morton was beheaded in 1581, Sir John Gordon of Haddo in 1644, President Spottiswoode in 1645, the Marquis of Argyll in 1661, and the Earl of Argyll in 1685; the Repentance Stool from Old Greyfriars' Church; John Knox's pulpit; the stool which the celebrated Jenny Geddes hurled at the head of the Dean of St Giles's when he essayed to read the Liturgy in St Giles's Church, Edinburgh, on the 23d July 1637; a banner of the Covenant used at the battle of Bothwell Brig in 1679; copies of the National Covenant, with the signatures of Montrose, Archbishop Leighton, and other Scottish nobles of the period; autographs of Queen Mary, her son James VI., Charles I., Cromwell, &c. &c.

The National Gallery.—(Admission—Mondays, Tuesdays, Wednesdays, and Saturdays from 10 till 5, and on Saturday evenings from 7 till 9, *free*—Thursdays and Fridays from 10 till 4, 6d. Catalogues 6d. Sticks and umbrellas must be left at the door, 1d). This handsome building occupies a site in the rear of the Royal Institution, and was also designed by Playfair. The foundation stone was laid by the late Prince Consort on the 30th of August 1850, and entirely finished in 1858, at a cost of nearly £40,000. The interior consists of two ranges of galleries, lighted entirely from the roof; in the eastern one the Royal Scottish Academy has its annual exhibitions of the works of living artists, and from February to May it is the most fashionable lounge in Edinburgh; the western one is assigned solely to the permanent collection of works of art. The first room contains specimens of the Flemish, Dutch, and French schools of the 16th and 17th centuries; the central or second room, specimens

, Genoese, Florentine, ₁ls of the same period ; devoted to specimens of

reet Gardens forms .de. At the top of the the gardens, just below lanade, stands an ancient te 5½ feet high, which n, and presented to the ₇87, who placed it here A serpent encircling an inscription in runic been translated thus— for Hialm his father ;

Ramsay. — Steell's f Allan Ramsay, author ral poem called "The ls in a fine position at Princes Street Gardens, the Royal Institution. which decorate the sides :, on the front, the late the Court of Session, nt at his own expense ; ₁, wife of the poet's son neral Ramsay, a grandhe east, Lady Campbell oet's granddaughters.—

tion of Scotland, e Insurance Association is in what is termed the joining it, on the west, is

irge and elegant edifice, loorway and projecting d by an association of for purposes similar to West End of London.

i in 1876, is a handsome ːes Street. It consists of nch style, on the ground ₁er on the upper floor, egant flight of steps.

iservative Club, a ited establishment, is at

r gentlemen engaged in es Street. And farther

Jlub, erected in 1866- £14,000. It is in the it details of a Grecian ite this building there is Brodie, R.S.A., of Sir rt., the discoverer of : agent.—A little farther

pal Chapel.—It was ːsign by W. Burn, and ₁ant specimen of the details after the model Windsor, it is an oblong

edifice, consisting of nave and aisles, 113 feet long and 62 feet wide, and is terminated at the western extremity by a square-pinnacled tower 120 feet high. The interior, which presents a most beautiful and imposing appearance, and contains a very fine organ, is adorned with a number of richly-coloured stained-glass windows, the great eastern one being 30 feet high, and containing figures of the twelve apostles, by Ballantine & Son of this city. The late incumbent here was Dean Ramsay, the genialhearted author of "Reminiscences of Scottish Life and Character," and one of the ablest and most distinguished clergymen connected with the Episcopal Church in Scotland. In the buryingground attached to the chapel repose the ashes of a number of eminent persons—Sir Henry Raeburn, the prince of Scottish portrait-painters ; the Rev. Arch. Alison, the well-known author of "Essays on Taste," and father of the historian of Europe ; Dr William Pulteney Alison, eldest son of the above, and brother of the historian, Professor successively of the Theory and Practice of Physic in the University, author of works of the highest authority in medical science, and one of the most philanthropic men that ever adorned the medical profession, of which he was long at the head in Edinburgh, and the able antagonist of Dr Chalmers in advocating the enforcement of a compulsory assessment for the support of the poor, in opposition to the doctor's voluntary one ; James Donaldson, founder of the magnificent hospital that bears his name ; the Rev. Dr Andrew Thomson, the first minister of St George's Church in Charlotte Square, and the most popular clergyman of his day ; Sir William Hamilton, Professor of Moral Philosophy in the University, and a philosopher of European fame ; Miss Catherine Sinclair, the well-known authoress ; Macvey Napier, who succeeded Lord Jeffrey as editor of the *Edinburgh Review ;* Sir William Arbuthnot, Lord Provost of Edinburgh in 1823 : and a number of others distinguished for their rank and learning. Beside St John's, there is a memorial stone, in the form of a Runic Cross, in recognition of Dean Ramsay.—Nearly opposite, in the centre of the public way, is

The Sinclair Fountain, a neat triangular structure, erected in 1859, by donation of Miss Catherine Sinclair, the authoress of "Modern Accomplishments," &c., a most benevolent lady, and for many years one of the most distinguished members of Edinburgh society. —A little to the south-west is

The New Station of the Caledonian Railway Company.—The present spacious buildings—which have been erected at a cost of upwards of £10,000, and the main front of which, to Princes Street, presents a one-story elevation, 103 feet long, and 22 feet high—are merely temporary erections.—A little farther south, in the hollow to the left, is

St Cuthbert's Parish Church.—It is one of the largest places of worship in Edinburgh, being seated for about 3000 persons. A church has occupied this site for more than a thousand years, but the present structure dates no farther back than 1775, the main edifice having been then erected at a cost of upwards of £4000, and a spire added some years afterwards at a separate cost. At the base of the spire is a fine piece of monumental sculpture from the chisel of the late Handyside Ritchie, in memory of the Rev. Dr David Dickson, who was minister of the parish for forty years. The surrounding cemetery contains the ashes of Napier of Merchiston, the inventor of logarithms, who was buried in a vault under the former church here in April 1617; and Thomas de Quincey, the eccentric "English Opium-Eater." The tomb is reached by taking the first pathway to the right at the Lothian Road entrance, and proceeding onward till a turn to the left is reached. On one of the south walls here, where it has hung for more than half a century almost unnoticed, there is a very beautiful piece of monumental sculpture by Flaxman. "It is a square architectural wall monument in that sort of mixed Roman and Grecian style prevalent at the end of the last and beginning of the present century, and was erected to commemorate the death of three infant children. The relievo, which forms the centre and ornament of the structure, is of the sharp oval shape common in classical monuments, about four feet high by two feet wide in the centre, and is of white statuary marble on a square slab of black marble. The chief figure is a full-length Christ; in action and expression full of mingled majesty and sweetness. The face is rather conventional, or seems so now, as it has suffered considerably from 'Time's effacing fingers;' but the figure has an air of gentleness and quiet dignity, combined with manly strength, fully indicative of the sculptor's easy command of his art, and his power of conveying the desired sentiment by the most simple means. The action of the right arm is that of leading, and as it falls by the side the hand is affectionately clasped and kissed by a child of about three years of age, whose tiny head just reaches it easily; the left lightly touches rather than rests upon the heads of two younger children, babies of little more than a year old, who are seated, embracing each other in a very natural attitude of infantile fondling. The quiet antique grace of the whole is a striking example of the consecrating power of genius; a story of ordinary sorrow is here so fully, beautifully, and unaffectedly recorded as to touch us still, and the memory of the infant sleepers is preserved by a stranger when those who loved them are probably themselves forgotten."—*Scotsman*. This exquisite piece of art having fallen into decay from long exposure, was recently removed, renovated, and replaced with loving skill and care, and entirely at his own expense, by a man of kindred genius, William Brodie, R.S.A. It is on the south-east end of the wall on the top of the rising ground, in a line almost due south from the base of the spire, and is reached by ascending the stone steps in the pathway a little to the south-west of the spire.—Leaving the churchyard, and entering Castle Terrace, the farther of the two roads on the left, a few paces bring us to

St. Mark's Chapel, erected in 1835, and the only Unitarian place of worship in Edinburgh. It has a somewhat elegant interior, and possesses a very fine organ.—As we proceed eastward, we catch a glimpse of the **Gaelic Free Church**, in a bye-street, and then stand in front of the **Offices of the U.P. Church**, originally erected as a **Theatre**. The adjoining tenement of dwelling-houses is a striking feature of this locality.—A little farther on, on the left, we cross King's Bridge, and proceed eastward by the road which sweeps past the base of the Castle rock. The first noticeable building we reach on the right is

The Normal School, in connection with the Church of Scotland. It was erected in 1845, at a cost of about £10,000. Visitors admitted on Tuesdays and Fridays.—Adjoining, on the east, is

St Columba's Episcopal Chapel, a neat little structure erected in 1846.—Crossing to the left we ascend a flight of stairs and speedily reach the Castle Hill.

CARVED STONE OVER ENTRANCE TO ROYAL APARTMENTS IN THE CASTLE.

THE CASTLE.

The Castle, perched on the summit of a rock some 443 feet above the level of the sea, forms the most prominent feature in all views of the city, and, next to Holyrood Palace, is the place which most interests strangers. This rock was the site of a stronghold long before the authentic records of Scottish history; but none of the present buildings, with the exception of the little Norman chapel of Queen Margaret, dates farther back than the fifteenth century.

EAST FRONT OF THE CASTLE IN 1573.

The Castle in 1573.—Previous to the memorable siege of 1573, when the gallant Kirkaldy of Grange held the Castle for Queen Mary and defended it for thirty-three days against the Regent Morton and the English auxiliaries under Sir William Drury, the eastern front of the fortress towards the city presented a very different appearance from what it now does, and, as will be seen from our illustration, must have been far more grandly picturesque and striking. The principal and central object, says Mr W. Chambers, in an interesting paper on the subject, was a donjon or keep, rising 60 feet above the summit of the rock, and known by the name of David's Tower, having been erected by David II. between 1368 and 1371. From the palace, a curtain wall extended northward along the front of the rock to this tower, from which again it passed on in the same direction to a somewhat smaller tower, the remains of which still exist embedded in the present half-moon battery; onwards from this smaller one the wall went northwards till it reached another tower of greater importance, called the Constable's Tower, being the residence of that officer, and which rose 50 feet high from the rocky platform, exactly over the site of the present portcullis gate, and accessible by a stair ascending the face of the rock, which formed the sole means of reaching the citadel or upper platform of the Castle. In the siege above referred to, five batteries played for nine days upon the eastern front, and wrought such ruin that David's Tower and the Constable's being wholly beaten down, all passage out or in was debarred by the mass of *debris;* and the gallant Kirkaldy and his brave companions, when they surrendered, had to be let down over the front by a rope. The whole of the present eastern front was constructed by the Regent Morton immediately after the siege.

The Esplanade.—The only approach to the fortress is by a fine spacious glacis or esplanade on the east, measuring about 100 yards by about 120, and which, previous to 1753, was only a steep narrow ridge. It was also used for a long while as a place of public execution, and was the scene of the death of Lord Forbes, Lady Glammis (sister of the Earl of Angus), in 1538, ostensibly for having conspired the death of James V., but in reality from the malice of private enmity; several of the earlier Reformers also suffered here. The **Monument in the form of a Runic Cross,** which stands at the railed parapet on the north, was raised by the officers and soldiers of the 78th Highlanders, in memory of their comrades who fell in India in 1857-58, while aiding to suppress the Sepoy Mutiny. The one nearer the Castle is a **Bronze Statue,** by Campbell, **of Frederick, Duke of York and Albany, K.G.,** son of George the Third, erected in 1839.

VIEW OF THE CASTLE FROM THE SOUTH.

Passing the palisadoed outer barrier, we enter the fortress itself by a drawbridge which spans a deep dry fosse guarded by small flanking batteries. Beyond this is the Guard-house, and farther up the ascent is the Portcullis Gate, over which is the old State Prison, where the Marquis and the Earl of Argyll, Principal Carstares, Lord Balcarres, and many other illustrious captives have been confined. A few steps farther brings us to the artificers' workshops, and the Argyll Battery on the right. A little farther on, at the bottom of a roadway, is **The Armory**, which is capable of holding 30,000 stand of arms; and immediately behind is the Old Sally Port, to which Viscount Dundee scrambled up to hold a conference with the Duke of Gordon, before setting out for the North to raise the Highland Clans in favour of King James. Returning and ascending by the causewayed pathway, we pass **The Governor's House**, erected in the time of Queen Anne, and what are called the New Barracks, a lofty pile raised on the western side of the rock in 1796. The Citadel, or highest platform of the Castle, is reached, a little farther on, by an old arched gateway, to the left of which is a huge iron tank or cistern for supplying the garrison with water.

Queen Margaret's Chapel.—The small barn-like building that meets our eye on the height in front is one of the most interesting objects in the Castle; for it is the little Norman Chapel built by Queen Margaret (the Saxon wife of Malcolm Canmore), who died in 1093, and may be regarded as the smallest and most ancient chapel in Scotland, measuring, as it does, only 16 feet 6 inches by 10 feet 6 inches within the nave. After a long period of neglect, it was restored in 1853, under the superintendence of Mr Charles Billings, and adorned with three small stained-glass windows. The one in the chancel represents Margaret herself, her husband, Malcolm Canmore, with a spear in his hand, and their son David I. The west window contains a Latin inscription, stating that the Chapel was built by Margaret, Queen of Scotland, who died on the 10th of June 1093, and after having been neglected for a time was restored in 1853.

MONS MEG, FROM AN OLD SKETCH.

Mons Meg.—Opposite, on the King's Bastion, stands the famous piece of ordnance known as Mons Meg, which some allege to have been forged at Mons, in Belgium, in 1476; while others assert that it was fabricated in Galloway, and used by James II. at the siege of Thrieve Castle in 1455. But however that may be, it is known to have been employed by James IV. at the siege of Dumbarton in 1489, and at that of Norham Castle, on the Borders, in 1497. It burst when firing a salute in honour of the Duke of York in 1682; was removed to the Tower of London in 1754; but was restored to Scotland (mainly at the intercession of Sir Walter Scott) by command of King George IV. in 1829. This large cannon is formed of long pieces of malleable iron held together by strong hoops of the same material. It is 13 feet long, 20 inches in diameter, and weighs upwards of 5 tons. The view from the bastion where it stands is, perhaps, unsurpassed in Europe, embracing as it does a magnificent range of sea and land.

Leaving this, and turning in a S.E. direction, the Half-Moon Battery, constructed by the Regent Morton in 1574, faces us, in the neighbourhood of which is the electric apparatus that discharges the Time Gun.

The Ancient Palace.—Turning westwards, we pass into a quadrangle a hundred feet square, the buildings on the south and east sides of which formed for centuries the Royal Palace and stronghold of the kings and queens of Scotland. The east side is where the royal apartments were located, where a long line of sovereigns were born and lived and died, and where many a lawless deed was done.

Queen Mary's Room.—On the ground floor here, at the south-east corner of the quadrangle, is the room in which, on the 19th of June 1566, Queen Mary gave birth to James I. of England. A stone tablet over the arch of the old doorway, with the initials H. and M., inwrought for Henry and Mary, and the date 1566, commemorates this event (see page 17). The room itself, which is singularly irregular in form and very small, its greatest length being little more than eight feet, has undergone but little change. Some of the original wainscot panelling having been injured or removed, has been replaced in a very rude and inelegant fashion. The original ceiling, however, is still preserved, wrought in ornamental wooden panels, with the initials I.R and M.R. surmounted with the royal crown in alternate compartments. On the wall is the royal arms, beneath which is the following inscription:—

"Lord Jesu Christ, that crouit was with Thornse,
Preserbe the Birth, quhais Badgie heir is borne,
And send Hir Sonne successione, to Reigne stille,
Long in this Realme, if that it be thy will.
Als grant, O Lord, quhai eber of Hir proceed,
Be to Thy Honer, and Praise, sobied.
19th IVNII, 1566."

that it was his and no other man's son. Then turning to an English gentleman present, she said, 'This is the son who, I hope, shall first unite the two kingdoms of Scotland and England.' Sir William Stanley said, 'Why, madam, shall he succeed before your majesty and his father?' 'Alas!' answered Mary, 'his father has broken to me,' alluding to his joining the murderous conspiracy against Rizzio. 'Sweet madam,' said Darnley, 'is this the promise that you made, that you would forget and forgive all?' 'I have forgiven all,' said the queen, 'but will never forget. What if Fawdonside's [one of the conspirators] pistol had shot? [She had felt the cold steel on her bosom.] What would have become of him and me both?' 'Madam,' said Darnley, 'these things are past.' 'Then,' said the queen, 'let them go;'" and so ended this singular conversation.

The building on the south side of the quadrangle was in ancient times the **Great Hall of the Palace**, a magnificent apartment, 80 feet long, 33 broad, and 27 in height, lighted by tall mullioned windows from the south, with a ceiling of open timber archwork in the style of the Parliament House, each joint springing from a sculptured corbel-stone. It used to accommodate the Parliament of the kingdom, and was the scene of many royal banquets, one of the last of which took place on the occasion of the visit of Charles I. to his native kingdom in 1633. It is now used as the Garrison Hospital, and, what with intruding floors and partitions, plain small windows, and whitewash, has well nigh lost all trace of its former grandeur. The building on the north side has been recently remodelled after a design by Billings, and is occupied as barracks.

The Crown Room.—On the east side of the quadrangle is the Crown Room, where the ancient regalia of Scotland are preserved, and to which admittance may be had daily, *free*, from 12 till 3 P.M. These insignia of royalty consist of crown, sceptre, and sword of state. The crown, although part of it bears the initials of James V., is supposed to be as old as the days of Robert Bruce. The last monarch crowned with it was Charles II. The sceptre, which was made for James V., is of silver, double gilt, thirty-four inches in length, hexagonal in form, and surmounted with statues of the Virgin, St Andrew, and St James. The sword of state is an elegant piece of Italian workmanship, and was a present from Pope Julius II. to James IV., in the year 1507. These royal symbols, and the Lord Treasurer's rod of office which lies beside them, remained long forgotten in this room, locked up in diamonds, worn by Charles I. at his coronation at Holyrood in 1633.

Leaving the Castle, and retracing our steps towards the city, we enter

The Castle Hill, which, a century and-a-half ago, was one of the most aristocratic quarters of the old town. Here stood the palace of Mary of Guise, the mother of Queen Mary; here the great Marquis of Argyll had a mansion, and here dwelt the Earls of Cassilis, Leven, and Dumfries, Lords Holyroodhouse, Sempill, and Rockville, the Countess Dowager of Hyndford, and many others of like rank. The first house on the right, descending from the Castle, bears on the pediment of a dormer window the date 1630; and a cannon-ball, which may be seen sticking in the gable wall next the esplanade, is said to have been shot from the Castle in 1745, during the occupation of the town by Prince Charles Edward. Another house, the entrance to which is through a finely-moulded ancient Gothic doorway in **Blair's Close** (372), was formerly the town mansion of the Dukes of Gordon. Over the entrance is an ogee arch, in the tympanum of which is a somewhat rudely-sculptured coronet, flanked by two deer-hounds, the well-known supporters of the Gordon family. The last member of the family who resided here was the Lady Elizabeth Howard, daughter of the Duke of Norfolk, and first Duchess of Gordon, who died in 1732. The house was afterwards occupied by the Bairds of Newbyth; and here the well-known General Sir David Baird, the hero of Seringapatam, and conqueror of Tippoo Saib, was born and brought up. Another house in the same alley was the residence, in 1783, of John Grieve, Esq., Lord Provost of Edinburgh.—Immediately opposite, on the left, is

The Reservoir, by which the town is supplied with water, drawn principally from the Pentland Hills, about seven miles south of the city. On the outside it is one story in height, with a tower 40 feet high; within it has an area 110 feet long, 90 feet broad, and 30 feet deep, and is estimated to contain about two millions of gallons of water, which can be distributed through the city at the rate of upwards of 5000 gallons per minute.

On the east side of Ramsay Lane is **Short's Observatory**, which terminates in a tower commanding a magnificent view of the city and its surrounding scenery. It has been recently remodelled and fitted up by Mr W. D. Hart, philosophical instrument maker, of this city, and is now in almost perfect condition, containing, as it does, perhaps the largest and most complete set of scientific apparatus in the kingdom for the illustration of astronomical, optical, and general science. In addition to the large and powerful telescopes, there is a splendid collection of microscopes; and the dome of the tower is fitted up with an achromatic camera obscura, which affords one of the grandest and most attractive panoramic views in the world. Altogether, there is not, perhaps, a more interesting exhibition in the city; and considering the smallness of the price

charged for admission—6d.—no one should pass it without paying a visit.

Allan Ramsay's House.—At the east end of the Reservoir is Ramsay Lane, which leads to a small octagonal-shaped house, overlooking West Princes Street Gardens. This house was built by Allan Ramsay, the poet, whose

marble statue we noticed in Princes Street; and here he retired in his sixtieth year, and spent in this pleasant retreat the last twelve years of his life in ease and tranquil enjoyment; and here he died in 1758. The house passed to his son, a man of high mental culture, and portrait-painter to King George III. and his queen, who enlarged it, and built three additional ones to the eastward, which still exist bearing the name of Ramsay Garden. At his death, in 1784, the property went to his son, General John Ramsay, who, dying in 1845 without issue, left the house and a large fortune to Mr Murray of Henderland, to whose heirs it still belongs.—**The Original Ragged School**, which owes its existence to the philanthropic efforts of Dr Guthrie, occupies a site in this lane, and is well worth a visit.—Proceeding down the lane towards the Mound, we come to

The Free Church College, an elegant specimen of the Elizabethan, or English collegiate style of architecture. It was designed by W. H. Playfair, founded in 1846, and finished in 1850, at a cost of upwards of £30,000. It has an open quadrangle, with library hall, senate hall, and nine class-rooms. Its entire frontage is 165 feet; the square tower at the north-east corner is 96 feet high, and the two centre towers flanking the main entrance 121 feet high each. The library hall is adorned with a statue of its first principal, Dr Chalmers.—The stairs on the south side of the quadrangle lead to

The **Free Church Assembly Hall**, which was erected in 1858-9, at a cost of £7000. It occupies the site of the palace of Mary of Guise. The design was furnished by David Bryce, R.S.A., and the £7000 was collected by ladies belonging to the Free Church throughout Scotland. To the east of the College is a structure designed by Mr Cousins in the Scottish baronial style, which is occupied by the **National Security Savings Bank** and the **Offices of the Free Church**.

Retracing our steps, and ascending Ramsay Lane, we are again in the Castle Hill. The first alley to the east of the Lane is **Sempill's Close**, formerly the residence of Hugh, twelfth

LORD SEMPILL'S HOUSE—1638.

Lord Sempill, who commanded a wing of the royal army at Culloden. Over the entrance to a projecting stair is the pious inscription—"Praised be the Lord my God, my strength, and my Redeemer, A.D. 1638," with the device of an anchor entwined by an S. Over another door is the inscription—*Sedes manet optima cælo*, with the date and device repeated. A few paces below this, on the site now occupied by the Free Church Assembly Hall, stood the **Palace of Mary of Guise**, queen of James V., and mother of Queen Mary.—Opposite is

The **Victoria or Assembly Hall**, a fine decorated Gothic edifice, which was built in 1842-44, at a cost of £16,000, for the accommodation of the General Assembly of the Church of Scotland, and was designed by the late Gillespie Graham. The beautiful octagonal spire, which surmounts the massive tower at the main entrance, is 240 feet high, and forms a point in all views of the city.—A little to the south, at the head of the West Bow, is

St John's Free Church, which was built in 1847, from a design by Robert Hamilton; and the pulpit of which was for many years filled by Drs Guthrie and Hanna.

The **West Bow**, which took its name from an arch or bow in the city wall which crossed the street here, and formed the western gateway of the city, was formerly a place of some note, and was lined from top to bottom with lofty picturesque timber-fronted tenements, of which the tall pile still standing on the east side at the head is a fair specimen. It was at one time, before the formation of the North and South Bridges, the principal entrance to the city on the west, and has been ascended in various state pageants by Anne of Denmark, James I., and by James IV. and his bride, the Princess Margaret of England, attended by the Archbishop of York, the Bishop of Durham, the Earl of Surrey, and a numerous and noble retinue; by James VI. (the latter of whom, on the 20th of October 1579, was conducted up this narrow way under a canopy of purple velvet, the windows being hung with tapestry and pictures, and the street strewed with flowers; by Mary of Guise, and Charles I.; by Oliver Cromwell, Charles II., and James II.—Immediately opposite, on the left, is

Milne's Court (No. 517.)—The large stone land in front was erected in 1690; but a house on the north side of the court which was formerly the residence of the lairds of Comiston is of a much earlier date. Over the entrance to a stair on the south side is the inscription—"*Blessit be God in al his Giftis*," and the date 1580.—Immediately to the east of this is No. 501,

James's Court, which was built in 1725-27, and is interesting as having been the residence of Henry Home (Lord Kames), David Hume, Dr Blair, James Boswell of Auchinleck, Johnson's biographer, &c. It was in Boswell's house here that Dr Johnson resided when he visited Edinburgh in August 1773, and where he met the *élite* of Edinburgh society. "Johnson and I," says Boswell, "walked arm-in-arm up the High Street, to my house in James's Court;" and as we went, "he acknowledged that the breadth of the street, and the loftiness of the buildings on each side, made a noble appearance." "My wife had tea ready for him," he adds, "and we sat chatting till near two in the morning."—Nearly opposite on the right, No. 322, is

Riddle's Close.—It was inhabited at one time by Bailie Macmoran, one of the magistrates of Edinburgh in the reign of James VI., and the greatest merchant of his day, and who was shot dead by one of the High School boys during a barring-out or rebellion in 1598. The principal room of his house, in which James VI. and his queen, Anne of Denmark, and her brother the Duke of Holstein, were entertained by the city of Edinburgh in 1597, is now used as the Mechanics' Library. Riddle's Close still contains, also, the houses occupied by Sir John Smith, Provost of Edinburgh in 1650; by David Hume, who wrote part of his history here; by Sir Roderick Mackenzie of Prestonhall, Lord Royston, Professor Pillans, &c.—On the opposite side is No. 469,

Baxter's Close, where Burns resided on his first visit to Edinburgh in November 1786. He shared an apartment with an acquaintance, John Richmond, a writer's clerk, the weekly rent of which was three shillings sterling. The house is on the first floor of the stair to the left, on entering the close.—A few paces to the east is No. 477,

Lady Stair's Close.—In the first floor of a house a little way down this close, on the left, the Dowager Countess of Stair resided for many years, when at the head of fashionable society in Edinburgh. Over the entrance doorway is the pious inscription—"Feare the Lord, and depart from Evill," with the date 1622, and the arms and initials of its original owners, Sir William Gray of Pittendrum, one of the merchant princes of old Edinburgh—the ancestor of the present Lord Gray—and Geida, his wife, sister of Sir John Smith of Grothill, Lord Provost of Edinburgh. Lady Stair afterwards became the wife of Viscount Primrose; and the romantic incidents of this period of her life form the groundwork of Scott's striking story of "My Aunt Margaret's Mirror."—To the east of this is Bank Street, at the foot of which stands

The Bank of Scotland.—It is the oldest banking establishment in Scotland, having been incorporated by Act of the Scottish Parliament in 1695. The original building was erected in 1806, from a design by Richard Crichton, at a cost of about £75,000; but recently two wings have been added, and the whole building externally renovated, after designs, in the Italian style, by David Bryce, R.S.A. The length of the façade is 175 feet, the height of the cupola from the pavement in Bank Street is 112 feet, of the campanile towers 90 feet, and of the main body of the building 55 feet. The most imposing feature of the present structure is the great central dome, the apex of which is crowned with a striking and graceful figure of Fame, which is 7 feet in height, cast in zinc, and gilded. With a paid-up capital of £1,000,000, the Bank has 1389 partners, and 75 branches.

Immediately opposite Bank Street is

George IV. Bridge, built in 1825-36, proceeding along which, and passing Victoria Street, and **The Highland and Agricultural Society's Chambers**, built in 1839, we notice, on the right, the battlemented steeple of a quaint old church in the valley below, called

The Magdalen Chapel.—It was erected prior to the Reformation (probably in 1503) by a pious citizen, Michael Macquhan, and Jonet Rhine, his widow, whose tomb is still shown in the floor. The windows of this ancient chapel are adorned with the oldest specimens of stained glass in Scotland, and the deep ruby and bright yellow of which, after the lapse of 360 years, still exhibit the unrivalled brilliancy of the old glass-painter's work. Here, in 1660, John Craig, the distinguished reformer and colleague of Knox, preached for some time in Latin, having, during an enforced absence of twenty-four years from his native land, lost the free use of his vernacular tongue; and here, in April 1578, the first General Assembly held after the Reformation had its first meeting-place, when "Mr Andro Melvill was chosin moderator," and "whar it was concludit, that bischoppes sould be callit be thair awin names, or be the names of *breither*, in all tyme coming, and that lordlie name and authoritie banissed frae the kirk of God, qwhilk hes bot ae Lord, Chryst Jesus." And it was to this quaint little sanctuary, so rich in old panellings, pious mottoes,

"And storied windows richly dight,
Casting a dim religious light,"

that the body of the martyred Marquis of Argyll was brought after his execution on the 27th of May 1661, to remain for a while till removed to the place of family sepulture at Kilmun. The chapel is now the property of the Protestant Institute of Scotland, on application to whose officer, at the rooms of the Institute, visitors are admitted to see the chapel *without fee*.—On the opposite side is the recently erected

Sheriff-Court Buildings.—This imposing structure is in the Italian style of architecture and was finished in 1868, after designs by David Bryce, R.S.A., at a cost of upwards of £44,000. —To the south of this, on the same side, is

St Augustine Church, the principal Congregationalist place of worship in Edinburgh. It was built in 1861, in the Byzantine style, from a design by Hay of Liverpool, and cost about £14,000.—Nearly opposite is

The Protestant Institute of Scotland, erected in 1860 by public subscription, to commemorate the ter-centenary of the Reformation.—A little to the South is **Martyrs' Free Church** (Dr Goold's).—At the extreme south end of the Bridge, on the right, is the entrance to

The Old and the New Greyfriars' Churches.—The one facing the entrance gate is the Old, the other, to the west, is the New. They are clumsy Gothic structures, destitute of any architectural adornment. The Old was opened in 1612, and the New in 1721. It was within the walls of the Old Church, on the 1st of March 1638, after a solemn sermon by the celebrated Alexander Henderson, that the great National Covenant was signed by the leading lords and barons of the realm. It was then carried out and placed on a neighbouring flat tombstone, where it was subscribed by the common people, many of whom, in their earnestness and zeal, used for the purpose their own blood instead of ink.

THE OLD CHURCH IN WHICH THE NATIONAL COVENANT WAS SIGNED.

The Old Church was burned down in 1845, but was restored a few years afterwards at considerable expense, and adorned with a number of beautiful memorial windows, the triplet one, in the south aisle, facing the entrance door, being to George Buchanan, the historian.

The pulpit of the Old Greyfriars' has been filled by some of the ablest men the Church of Scotland has produced. Robert Rollock, the first principal of the University of Edinburgh; Principal Carstares, the friend of King William, and one of the prominent men of his time; Principal Robertson, the historian; Dr John Erskine, the son of Erskine of Cardrock, the learned author of "The Institutes of the Law of Scotland," and one of the most distinguished clergymen of his day; Dr John Inglis, long leader of the moderate party in the Church of Scotland, author of an able work on the "Evidences of Christianity," and father of the Right Hon. John Inglis of Glencorse, the present Lord President of the Court of Session; Dr Guthrie, and Dr Robert Lee, have all been incumbents here.

And it is to this interesting old church that Scott—who had worshipped in it when a boy, and whose father and several of his family are buried in the adjoining grounds—makes Counsellor Pleydell, in "Guy Mannering," conduct Colonel Mannering to hear the most distinguished clergyman of his day, the "historian of Scotland, of the Continent, and of America." "But they were disappointed—he did not preach that morning. 'Never mind,' said the counsellor; 'have a moment's patience, and we shall do very well.' The colleague of Dr Robertson ascended the pulpit [Dr John Erskine]. His external appearance was not prepossessing. 'The preacher seems a very ungainly person,' whispered Mannering to his new friend. 'Never fear; he's the son of an excellent Scottish lawyer; he'll show blood, I'll warrant him.' The learned counsellor predicted truly;" for "Mannering had seldom heard so much learning, metaphysical acuteness, and energy of argument, brought into the service of Christianity. 'Such,' he said, going out of the church, 'must have been the preachers to whose unfearing minds, and acute, though sometimes rudely exercised talents, we owe the Reformation.'"

The Greyfriars' Churchyard is one of the most interesting places of sepulture in Scotland. It was originally a garden belonging to a community of Grey Friars, whose monastery, founded by James I., between 1424 and 1437, was situated on the south side of the Grassmarket, fronting the foot of the West Bow. This monastery was destroyed in 1559, and every vestige of it has long since disappeared. The garden passed into the possession of the Town Council in 1561, and a few years afterwards it was, by special grant of Queen Mary, constituted the city cemetery. Here, on the 2d of June 1581, wrapped up in a coarse cloak, and carried under night by the rude hands of the common porters of the city, was brought the headless body of the once powerful Regent Morton, after his execution by the Maiden, and secretly buried in a nameless and obscure grave. Here, also, lie the remains of George Buchanan, the celebrated Latin scholar and his-

HENDERSON'S MONUMENT.

torian; Alexander Henderson, the leading delegate from Scotland to the great Westminster Assembly of Divines, and the principal author of the Assembly's Catechism; George Jamesone, who is supposed to have been the first native Scots painter, and who studied under Rubens, at Antwerp; Robert Mylne, master mason to several of the Scottish kings, and who built a large portion of Holyrood Palace, and several old buildings bearing his name in the city; Thos.

Ruddiman, the distinguished philologist and grammarian; Sir George Mackenzie of Rosehaugh, the king's advocate in the persecuting times of Charles II. and James II.; and such was the

MACKENZIE'S MONUMENT.

detestation inspired in the popular mind by his cruel and time-serving persecution of the Covenanters, that it was commonly believed his body could not rest in the grave, and the urchins of the town were wont to amuse themselves by shouting at the key-hole of his mausoleum—

"Bluidy Mackenzie, come out if ye daur;
Lift the sneck, and draw the bar!"

Allan Ramsay, the poet; William Ged, the inventor of stereotyping; Duncan Forbes of Culloden, Lord President of the Court of Session; Lord President Blair; the two Munros, Professors of Anatomy; Dr Joseph Black, the celebrated chemist; Dr Robertson and Patrick Fraser Tytler, the historians; Henry Mackenzie, "The Man of Feeling;" John Kay, the celebrated caricaturist; Dr Hugh Blair, Dr M'Crie, the biographer of John Knox; thirty-seven chief magistrates of the city are also interred here; twenty-three principals and professors of the University, many of them the most distinguished men of their age; thirty-three of the most eminent lawyers of their day—one of them Vice-Chancellor of England, and Master of the Rolls, another Accountant-General of the Court of Chancery, six of them Lords President of the Supreme Court of Scotland, and twenty-two Senators of the College of Justice; and many other persons distinguished for their rank or genius. In the north end of the east street wall, is the Martyrs' Monument, which marks the spot where the greater number of the Covenanters are interred who were executed in Edinburgh during the reigns of Charles II. and James II. It contains the following inscriptions:—

"Halt, passenger, take heed what you do see—
This tomb doth shew for what some men did die:
Here lies interr'd the dust of those who stood
'Gainst perjury, resisting unto blood;
Adhering to the covenants and laws;
Establishing the same; which was the cause
Their lives were sacrific'd unto the lust
Of prelatists abjured: though here their dust
Lies mixt with murderers and other crew,
Whom justice justly did to death pursue.
But as for them no cause was to be found
Worthy of death; but only they were found
Constant and stedfast, zealous, witnessing
For the prerogatives of Christ their King;
Which truths were seal'd by famous Guthrie's head,
And all along to Mr Renwick's blood:
They did endure the wrath of enemies:
Reproaches, torments, deaths, and injuries.
But yet they're those, who from such troubles came,
And now triumph in glory with the Lamb."

"From May 27, 1661, that the most noble Marquis of Argyle was beheaded, to the 17th February 1688, that Mr James Renwick suffered, were one way or other murdered and destroyed for the same cause about eighteen thousand, of whom were executed at Edinburgh about an hundred of noblemen, gentlemen, ministers, and others, noble martyrs for Jesus Christ. The most of them lie here."

THE MARTYRS' MONUMENT, WITH THE SPIRES OF MAGDALEN CHAPEL AND ST GILES'S.

In a recess on the south side of the grave-yard in June 1679 about 1200 Covenanters, taken prisoners at Bothwell Bridge, were confined for five months, unhoused and almost unfed.

Lord Brougham's Birthplace.—Leaving the churchyard, and turning to the left, we proceed down the Candlemaker Row, at the bottom of which, on the north side of the Cowgate, a few paces to the west of the church, is a tall stone land, in a room on the third floor of which Lord Brougham was supposed to have been born in 1778. The mistake probably arose from his lordship's father having resided here for a year or two prior to his marriage. The future Lord Chancellor was born in the top floor of the corner house on the north side of St Andrew Square (now numbered 21), on the 19th of September 1778.—Turning to the left, and proceeding a few paces westward, the Tourist enters

The Grassmarket.—A weekly market has been held here since 1477. The New Corn Exchange, on the south side, was erected in 1849, after a design by David Cousin, at a cost of nearly £20,000. It is in the Italian style, with a front of three storeys, and a campanile or belfry at the north end. This spacious street was for centuries the place of public execution, and has been the scene of some memorable historical events. Here, during the persecuting times of Charles II. and James II., Montrose and Argyll, and a great host of Covenanters, witnessed a good confession; and here, too—the street "crowded with rioters, crimson with torch-light, spectators filling every window of the tall houses"—the unfortunate Captain Porteous met his doom at the hands of an infuriated rabble, "the Castle standing high above the tumult, against the blue midnight and the stars." The spot where the executions took place is at the east end, near the foot of the West Bow, and is now marked by a cross in the causeway.—At the west end is

The West Port, which was originally a village under the name of Portsburgh. Its present name was derived from a gateway in the city wall, at its east end. Retracing our steps, we ascend the West Bow, and pass up Victoria Street, noticing on the right a massive pile of buildings in the old Scottish or baronial style, erected in 1867-68, by Messrs Charles Lawson & Sons, seed merchants, as business premises, and called **India Buildings.** The interior of this imposing erection is of unique construction, each of the numerous offices being self-contained, and entering from a series of circular galleries amply lighted from the roof.

Passing along Melbourne Place, on the right, immediately behind the County hall, there still exists a part of the "transs" of **Libberton's Wynd,** at one time one of the principal thoroughfares for pedestrians from the fashionable district of the Cowgate to the "High Town." Here, during the greater part of the last century, and a portion of the present, stood **John Dowie's Tavern,** a well-known house of public entertainment, erected in 1728, whither the chief wits and men of letters, lords of session, and leading advocates, were wont to resort, in accordance with the convivial habits of the times. Here Ferguson the poet, David Herd, the earliest collector of Scottish Songs, Martin, a celebrated portrait-painter of the last century, and Sir Henry Raeburn, his still more celebrated pupil, and Burns, with many others, spent many jovial hours. At the head of this wynd, three reversed stones in the causeway indicate the spot where the last sentence of the law was wont to be carried out—the place of common execution.—Adjoining, on the east, is

The County Hall, erected in 1816-19, in the Grecian Doric style, from a design by Archibald Elliot, at a cost of £15,000. It is architecturally interesting as having been built after the plan of the Temple of Erechtheus at Athens, while the principal entrance is an imitation of the Choragic monument of Thrasyllus. On the opposite side is No. 413, **Dunbar's Close,** where Cromwell's "Ironsides" had their guard-house and took up their quarters after the victory of Dunbar, from which circumstance the close was named.

A little to the east of this, and a yard or two from the north-west corner of St Giles's, a heart-figure in the pathway, centred with the veritable stone that indicated the market cross for 200 years, marks the site of **The Old Tolbooth,** a grim dismal-looking five-storied pile of tower and turret that stood here for over 300 years, and

THE OLD TOLBOOTH.

the scene of many important historical events. After having served as a hall for the national Parliaments, as a meeting-place for the Supreme Court of the country, and for some of the earliest assemblies of the Kirk, it latterly degenerated into the prison of the old Scottish capital, and the north gable of which appears to have been the place of exposure for the heads and dismembered limbs of the numerous victims of the sanguinary laws of early times. Here, in 1581, the head of the Regent Morton was fixed upon an iron spike, which was followed in 1650 by that of the gallant Marquis of Montrose, and in 1661 by that of the Marquis of Argyll. "The Heart of Midlothian," as it was popularly called, and which has been immortalised in Scott's delightful novel of the same name, in connexion with the Porteous riot, one of the most daring popular tumults that ever took place in the city,* was taken down in 1817.

St Giles's Cathedral forms the principal ornament of the High Street. It is a large decorated Gothic edifice in the form of a cross, with a massive central square tower, terminating in open stone work, in the form of an imperial crown, surmounted by a light and graceful spire springing from a cluster of pinnacles, and rising to the height of 161 feet from the ground. The original church is said to have been founded here early in the 9th century; but the first mention of it in any authentic record does not occur till the reign of Alexander II. in 1214. It is again mentioned in an act of the reign of Robert the Bruce in 1319; and, still later, mention is made of additions to the original foundation in a charter of David II.'s in 1359. In 1466, at which period there were no fewer than forty altars within its walls, and a holy relic, in the shape of an armbone of St Giles enshrined in a silver case, James III. made it a collegiate church, with an establishment consisting of a provost, sixteen prebendaries, a curate, a minister of the choir, four choristers, a sacristan, and a beadle. Gawin Douglas, the famous Scottish poet, author of "The Palice of Honor," and translator of the

---

* Captain John Porteous, commander of the city guard, having had occasion to quell some disturbances at the execution of a smuggler of the name of Wilson, in the Grassmarket, on the 14th of April 1736, rashly ordered his soldiers to fire upon the crowd, by which six were killed and eleven wounded, including some females and a number of the spectators from the neighbouring windows. For this Porteous was tried and condemned to death for murder, but was reprieved by Queen Caroline, who was then acting as Regent, in the absence of her husband, George II., at Hanover. The people, however—who had regarded Wilson in the light of a victim to the oppressive excise laws, and other fruits of the detested Union—were so exasperated at the pardon of one who had murdered in cold blood so many of their fellow-citizens, that they determined he should not escape. Accordingly, on the evening of 7th September 1736, which was the day previous to that which had been appointed for Porteous's execution, and when, confident of his speedy deliverance, he was feasting a party of his friends in his apartment in the prison, a large and disorderly assemblage collected in a district called Portsburgh. and proceeded by tuck of drum to the Old Tolbooth, gradually augmenting their numbers as they went. On arriving there, they surprised the town guard, armed themselves with their weapons, and, after vainly thundering at the massive doors for a time with sledge hammers, forced them at length by fire, and rushing in with yells of fury, dragged their trembling victim, all begrimed with soot, from the chimney of his apartment, whither he had vainly fled for refuge. After permitting him to intrust what money or papers he had about him to a friend for behoof of his family, they conducted him, in a sort of rude torch-light procession, borne on the shoulders of two of the rioters, and guarded by a band armed with muskets and battleaxes, up the Lawnmarket and down the West Bow, to the place of common execution in the south-east corner of the Grassmarket, and which is still marked by a cross in the causeway; and there, at midnight, in "the wild lurid street, crowded with rioters, crimson with torch-light, spectators filling every window of the tall houses, and the Castle standing high above the tumult against the blue midnight and the stars," they led him to a death as ignominious as it was lingering and cruel, for, hastily throwing a rope round his neck, they suspended him to a dyer's pole, and left him there making frantic efforts to get hold of the beam from which he hung.

"Æneid" into Scottish verse, was provost here in 1509. At the Reformation, the old establishment was abolished, and the building was divided into four separate places of worship. The section on the east of the transept, known at that time as St Giles's, but now as the High Church, became the parish church of Edinburgh, and John Knox was appointed pastor. Here, in July 1565, he delivered one of his boldest and most vehement harangues on the subject of Mary's marriage with Darnley, in which, with especial indignation, he denounced the nobles and other leaders of the congregation as betraying the cause of God by their inaction in the matter. "I see," said he, suddenly stretching out his arms, as if he

KNOX PREACHING IN ST GILES'S.

would leap from the pulpit, and arrest the passing vision, "I see before me your beleaguered camp. I hear the tramp of the horsemen as they charged you in the streets,"—and in a strain of lofty and sustained eloquence he denounced, exhorted, and warned his hearers, with such vehemence, says Melvil, that, "he was like to ding [dash] the pulpit in blads [splinters] and flee out of it!" And it was here, on Sunday the 3d of April 1603, that James VI. attended divine service, and took farewell of his people, before setting out for England. Here, also, from the royal seat in the gallery, the king was wont, occasionally, to administer rebukes to offensive clergymen; for we read that in 1586, when Mr Walter Balcanquall, a relative of George Heriot's, was preaching before his majesty, in "the Great Kirk of Edinburgh," he said something against Episcopacy, for which the king, "after sermoun, rebooked Mr Walter publiclie from his seat in the loaft, and said he would prove there sould be bishoppes," &c. When Edinburgh was erected into a diocese by Charles

I. in 1633, St Giles's was constituted the Cathedral Church, and continued so for six years, until Cromwell overturned Episcopacy. It regained

WEST SIDE OF ST GILES'S.

its episcopal dignity at the Restoration, but lost it again by the Revolution of 1688. It was in the Old Church division, at the south end of the transept, that, on the 23d of July 1637, the redoubted Jenny Geddes hurled her stool at the head

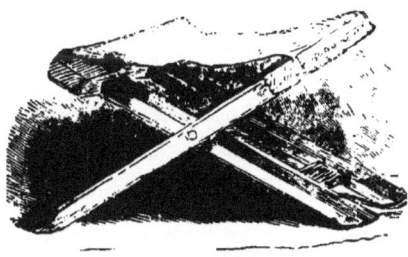

JENNY GEDDES'S STOOL.

of the Dean of Edinburgh, when he essayed to read the collect for the day, exclaiming, as she did so, "Colic, said ye? the Deil colic the wame o' ye! Wud ye say mass at my lug?' This raised such a storm against the introduction of Episcopacy into Scotland, that no further attempt was made to impose the liturgy upon the people. Here, too, on the 13th of October 1643, the Solemn League and Covenant was sworn to and subscribed by the Committee of Estates of Parliament, the Commission of the Church, and the English Commission. This same Old Church portion is also celebrated as being the place of sepulture of the Regent Moray, who was assassinated at Linlithgow, by Hamilton of Bothwellhaugh in 1570, of the Earl of Athole, Chancellor of the kingdom, who died in April 1579, and of the famous Marquis of Montrose, who was executed in 1650. For many years after this period the old building was abandoned to sundry ignoble uses not at all in keeping with its sacred character. Internally, it was sometimes used as a meeting-place for the General Assembly, sometimes employed as a Council-Chamber, and at other times as a prison; while externally its walls were plastered round about with a number of booths or shops, after the fashion of cobblers' stalls, in which the occupants not only plied their trades, but lived with their families upon the premises. Down till 1829 the church consisted of a mass of Gothic buildings erected at

NORTH SIDE OF OLD ST GILES'S PREVIOUS TO 1829.

different times without regard to harmony of style; but in 1830-32, with the aid of a Government grant of £10,000, the whole structure was "renovated," as it is called, after a design by Mr Burn, in what is termed the decorated Gothic style. The church as it now stands is the work of many different periods; but no part of its architecture indicates an earlier date than the 14th century. The oldest external portion is the spire, which was erected in 1648, on the model of a previous one. The interior has recently been entirely reconstructed at an expense of £30,000 by the late Dr. William Chambers, the Publisher, who for several years was Lord Provost of the city. Since this restoration, most of the windows have been filled in with stained glass, and mural brasses have been erected in memory of Edinburgh citizens and other public persons, less or more connected with the Church and its history.

PARLIAMENT HOUSE
ABOUT 1646.

The **Parliament Square** was used from an early period to the end of the sixteenth century as a public cemetery. From that time to the present, however, it has been devoted to buildings chiefly connected with the Courts of Law. On the south-east side are the Exchequer Offices and the Union Bank. The south side is occupied by the Court of Justiciary, the Chambers of Her Majesty's Board of Works, and the Court of Session; on the west is the Signet Library. **An Equestrian Statue of Charles II.** in bronzed lead, erected by the Magistrates and Council in 1685, at an expense of £215, occupies the centre of the square.

John Knox's Grave.—A few paces to the west of this, a small surface-bronzed stone in the ground, with the initials J. K. (John Knox), indicates the spot where, on the 26th of November 1572, the assembled nobles and citizens committed all that was mortal of the great Reformer to the grave, the Regent Morton pronouncing over him the memorable eulogium—"There lies he who never feared the face of man!"—Immediately opposite, on the south, is the entrance to

The Parliament House, one of the most interesting public buildings in Edinburgh. It was erected in 1631-36, at an expense of £11,600. As will be seen from our illustration, the original structure—the design of which tradition assigned to Inigo Jones—had a quaint stateliness about its antique turrets and sculptures, its irregular pinnacles and towers, and the rude elaborateness of its decorations, that gave it a highly picturesque appearance, thoroughly in accordance with the age in which it was erected, which is wholly wanting in the present façade, with its mixed features of arcade, piazza, portico, and balustrade. The last Parliament held here was on the 25th of March 1707, when the Treaty of Union was ratified, and the legislature of Scotland adjourned, never again to assemble—the Lord Chancellor Seafield, who presided, exclaiming, "There's an end of an auld sang!" After that event, the building was assigned to the Court of Session, or Supreme Court of Scotland, which formerly met in the Old Tolbooth.

The Great Hall in which the Parliament met is a magnificent apartment, 122 feet in length, 40 feet in breadth, and upwards of 60 feet in height, with a pendent oaken roof, springing from a series of grotesquely, yet elegantly sculptured corbels of various designs, and similar in character to that of Westminster Hall. With the exception of the royal apartments in Holyrood, there is no other place in the city so rich in historic memories as this grand old hall, the scene of the latest legislative assemblies of the country, and the arena of debate of the leading Scottish nobles and statesmen of the last two centuries. "Here," says one of its latest chroniclers, "Montrose united with Rothes, Lindsay, Loudon, and the other Covenanting leaders, in maturing the bold measures that formed the basis of our national liberties; and within the same hall, only a few years later, he sat with the calmness of despair to receive from the lips of his old compatriot, Loudon, the barbarous sentence which was executed with such savage rigour." Here, too, in those times of persecution and civil strife, James Duke of York presided, along with Dalziell and Graham of Claverhouse, to try, by browbeating and torture, the passive heroism of the confessors of the Covenant, and to consign, without form of trial, to the dungeon and the scaffold, such men as Guthrie, and Argyll, and hundreds of lesser note; while Sir George Mackenzie, "that noble wit of Scotland," as Dryden terms him, played the part of king's advocate with such persecuting zeal as to earn for himself the more enduring and popular title of "bluidy Mackenzie." In this hall, also, on the 14th of August 1656, General Monk, Duke of Albemarle, was feasted in great state; here, too, the persecuting and bigoted James Duke of York, afterwards James VII., along with his Duchess, and the Lady Anne, afterwards Queen Anne, was entertained in princely fashion on his arrival in Edinburgh in 1680; and here, also, George IV. was received in kingly state at a grand banquet on his visit to the city in 1822. This great hall is now used as a waiting-room and promenade by the advocates and other practitioners connected with the Supreme Courts, and during the sitting of the courts presents a very attractive and animated scene

The Great Window.—The magnificent stained-glass window at the south end was erected in October 1868, at a cost of £2000. It is the work of two German artists, having been designed by W. von Kaulbach, and executed by the Chevalier Ainmiller of Munich. It represents the inauguration of the College of Justice, or the Supreme Court of Scotland, by King James V., in 1532. The opening of the court for the first time is supposed by the artist to have been the occasion of a grand state ceremonial; and the moment chosen for representation is that in which the youthful king, surrounded by his nobles and great officers of state, is supposed to be in the act of presenting the deed of institution to the Abbot of Cambuskenneth, the Lord President of the Court, who kneels before him to receive it, surrounded by the other judges in their robes; while the Lord Chancellor of Scotland, Dunbar, Archbishop of Glasgow, the chief ecclesiastic present, raises his hand to invoke a blessing on the act.

The Side Windows.—The four windows on the west side of the hall were, in the summer of 1870, under the superintendence of Sir George Harvey, President of the Royal Scottish Academy, filled in with stained glass of a heraldic character, executed by Messrs Ballantine & Son, of this city. Each window is about 20 feet high, and 9 feet wide, divided by a centre mullion into two lights with tracery, and contains in the main portion ten coats of arms, and in the tracery openings four crests. The first window (the one next the great window) contains the armorial bearings and crests of the LORDS JUSTICE-CLERK whose names are inscribed thereon; the second contains those of the GREAT LEGAL WRITERS of the Faculty of Advocates; the third, those of the DEANS OF FACULTY; and the fourth, those of the LORDS ADVOCATE.

The Faculty of Advocates.—The Faculty of Advocates—who are privileged to plead in any court in Scotland, and in all Scotch appeals before the House of Lords, and from amongst whom are selected the thirteen judges of the Supreme Court, and the sheriffs of the various counties—is the most distinguished corporate body in Scotland, and has always been composed of men representative alike of the rank and intellect of the country. For more than three hundred years the dignity of the Scottish bench and the honour of the Scottish bar have been upheld by a succession of distinguished men, illustrious not only in their own peculiar department of legal learning, but in every branch of literature, science, and art. And this grand old hall, whose "long array of mighty shadows" look out upon us from the marble, or down upon us from the canvas on its walls, has echoed to the tread of a long line of men whose works are read and whose influence is felt wherever the English language is known.

The Statues and Portraits.—The hall is adorned with a number of fine statues and busts, and the walls are hung with portraits, of distinguished statesmen and lawyers connected with the Scottish bench and bar. Of the statues, the most noticeable are, at the north end of the hall, a colossal one of Henry Dundas, the first Viscount Melville, in his robes as a peer, by Chantrey; on his left is Lord Cockburn, by Brodie; next to him is Duncan Forbes of Culloden, in his judicial costume as Lord President of the Court, by the celebrated French sculptor, Roubiliac; beyond him is Lord President Boyle, by Steel; and still farther up is Lord Jeffrey, also by Steell; next to him is Lord President Blair (the son of the author of "The Grave"), by Chantrey; and opposite him, on the other side of the hall, is the Right Hon. Robert Dundas of Arniston, Lord Chief Baron of the Scottish Exchequer, also by Chantrey. Of the portraits, perhaps the most striking is a full-length one of Lord Brougham, by Daniel Macnee, R.S.A.; another of Lord Colonsay, formerly Lord President of the Court, but now a peer of the realm; another and by the same artist, of Lord Justice-Clerk Hope; there are also two very fine half-length portraits of Lord Abercromby and Professor Bell by Sir Henry Raeburn; specimens by the celebrated Jamesone, the earliest Scottish painter, who studied under Rubens at Antwerp, &c.

The Courts.—The Court of Session is divided into what is called the Outer and the Inner House. The former consists of five Judges or Lords Ordinary, occupying separate courts, who hear cases for the first time; the latter comprises two courts, technically known as the First and Second Divisions. Four Judges sit in each Division, and it is before them that litigants, dissatisfied with the Outer House decisions, may bring their cases for final judgment, unless afterwards they have recourse to the expensive luxury of appealing to the House of Lords. The courts of the Lords Ordinary enter from the dimly-lighted corridor at the south end of the great hall, and those of the Inner House from the east lobby.—By a door on the west side of the hall entrance may be obtained to

The **Advocates' Library**, which was founded in 1682, at the suggestion of Sir George Mackenzie, then Lord Advocate. It is one of the five great libraries in the country entitled to a copy of every work printed in Britain, and contains over 200,000 printed volumes, and about 2000 manuscripts. Amongst its most interesting treasures are a beautiful copy of the first printed Bible, in black letter, from the press of Faust and Guttenburg, in 1450; a few Caxtons; first specimens of Scottish printing, 1508-1510; a manuscript copy of St Jerome's translation of the Scriptures, supposed to have been written in the tenth century, and known to have been used in the Abbey Church of Dunfermline in the reign of David I.; the original Confession of Faith, drawn up by John Craig, the colleague of Knox, and signed by James VI. in 1580; several original copies of the Solemn League and Covenant of 1638; the chartularies of many of the ancient religious houses; illuminated missals; the celebrated Wodrow manuscripts, relating to the ecclesiastical history of Scotland; the original manuscript of "Waverley," &c. Strangers are freely admitted to walk through the several apartments and view these curiosities. Thomas Ruddiman, the celebrated grammarian and critic; David Hume, and Adam Ferguson, the historians; and David Irving, LL.D., author of "Lives of Scottish Poets," and other works; Mr. Halkett, a distinguished linguist and bibliographer, and Mr. Jamieson, editor of "The Shyp of Fooles," have filled the office of librarian here.

The **Library of the Writers to the Signet** adjoins that of the Advocates. It is contained in a large edifice in the Grecian style of architecture, and may be entered either from the north end of the Parliament Hall or from the south side of the vacant space between St Giles's Church and the County Hall. This valuable library was founded in 1755, and consists of more than 60,000 volumes, which are chiefly contained in two magnificent halls, fitted up and adorned with busts and portraits. In the centre of the upper hall, 140 feet long and 42 feet wide, is a cupola, enriched with paintings from the pencil of the late Mr Stothard. The erection of the building cost the Society of Writers to the Signet £25,000. David Laing, LL.D., the well-known antiquary and bibliographer, is the present librarian.

On leaving the Signet Library, and passing into the High Street by the west side of St Giles's, on the left, is **Byres' Close**, No. 373, which contained the town mansion of Sir John Byres of Coates, erected in 1611; and which still contains a much older and more interesting mansion, that of the celebrated Adam Bothwell, Bishop of Orkney, and Commendator of Holyroodhouse, who, on the 15th of May 1567, in the Chapel Royal of Holyrood Palace, performed the marriage ceremony that gave Bothwell possession of the unfortunate Queen Mary. Two months afterwards, this timorous and time-serving prelate deserted his royal mistress, and placed the crown on the head of her infant son. The house presents a semi-hexagonal front to the north, and was originally surmounted by elegantly carved dormer windows, traces of which still remain, and anciently stood in the midst of a terraced garden

ADAM BOTHWELL'S HOUSE.

which has long since been swept away. In this house, too, dwelt the beautiful but unfortunate heroine of the fine old ballad of "Lady Anne Bothwell's Lament."

Immediately adjoining is No. 371, the shop of Messrs J. Clapperton & Co., and a place of some little interest, as having formerly been the business premises of Sir William Dick of Braid, Lord Provost of the city in 1638-39, an eminent public-spirited citizen and merchant, and reputed the wealthiest man of his time in Scotland, his fleets extending from the Baltic to the Mediterranean. The fore part of the ancient building has been entirely modernized and faced with a new stone front, but the body of the structure still remains intact. Sir William being a zealous Covenanter, advanced large sums of money to enable his party to withstand King Charles, who could not have been faced at Dunse Law but for the well-filled coffers of the wealthy merchant. Scott, in the "Heart of Midlothian," alludes to this latter incident, where he makes David Deans exclaim, "My father saw them toom the sacks of dollars out o' Provost Dick's window intil the carts that carried them to the army at Dunse Law; and if ye winna believe his testimony, there is the window itsell still standing in the Luckenbooths, five doors abune Advocates' Close—I think it's a claith-merchant's buith the day." And singularly enough a cloth-merchant's booth it continues to be. The wealthy provost, however, ultimately died in prison at Westminster, in want of even the common necessaries of life.

A little farther east is No. 357, **Advocates' Close**, a precipitous, gloomy-looking alley, which was formerly the residence of Lord Advocate Stewart, Lord Westhall, Andrew Crosbie, the Counsellor Pleydell of "Guy Mannering," and other distinguished lawyers. It is in this wretched-looking place that Scott makes Colonel Mannering, while in search of the counsellors' house, first encounter Dandie Dinmont. "His conductor hurried him across the High Street, and suddenly dived with him into a very steep paved lane [Advocates' Close]. Turning to the right, they entered a scale-staircase, as it is called, the state of which, so far as it could be judged of by one of his senses, annoyed Mannering's delicacy not a little. When they had ascended cautiously to a considerable height, they heard a heavy rap at a door, still two stories above them. The door opened, and immediately ensued the sharp and worrying bark of a dog, the scream of a woman, the squalling of an assaulted cat, and the hoarse voice of a man, who cried in a most imperative tone, 'Will ye, Mustard? will ye?—down, sir ! down !' 'Lord preserve us,' said the female voice, 'an he had worried our cat, Mr Pleydell would ne'er hae forgi'en me !' 'Aweel, my doo, the cat's no a prin the waur—So he's no in, ye say?' 'Na, Mr Pleydell's ne'er in the house on Saturday at e'en,' answered the female voice. 'And the morn's Sabbath, too,' said the querist, 'I dinna ken what will be done.' By this time Mannering appeared, and found a tall strong countryman, cla'l in a coat of pepper-and-salt coloured mixture, with huge metal buttons, a glazed hat and boots, and a large horse-whip beneath his arm, in colloquy with a slip-shod damsel, who had in one hand the lock of the door, and in the other a pail of whiting, or *camstane*, as it is called, mixed with water—a circumstance which indicates Saturday night in Edinburgh."

A little farther eastward is No. 341, **Roxburgh Close**, which derived its name from having formerly been the dwelling-place of the Earls of Roxburgh.—Still farther east is No. 323, **Warriston's Close**, which now retains hardly any trace of its ancient features, but which was formerly one of the most important alleys of the Old Town, and the residence of some of the most distinguished persons of their day, amongst whom were Sir Thomas Craig, a senator of the College of Justice, and his well-known nephew Sir Archibald Johnston of Warriston, who took so prominent a part in the resistance offered to the schemes of Charles I., Sir George Urquhart of Cromarty, Sir Robert Baird of Saughton Hall, and many others.—Immediately adjoining, on the east, is

No. 315, **Writers' Court**, which derives its name from the Signet Library having formerly been kept here. In this Court was situated Clerihugh's tavern, a celebrated place of convivial resort during the last century, and which still stands at the bottom of the court, though its deserted walls no longer ring with the revelry and mad merriment of former times. It was also the meeting-place of the "Mirror" Club, amongst the members of which were Henry Mackenzie, Lord Craig, Lord Abercromby, Lord Bannatyne, Lord Cullen, George Home of Wedderburn, &c. It is to this place, also, that Scott conducts Colonel Mannering and Dandie Dinmont, on a certain Saturday night, and describes them as turning into a dark alley, then up a dark stair, and into an open door, in search of Counsellor Pleydell, whom they find in the midst of a jovial company closely engaged in the enjoyment of the ancient but now forgotten pastime of *High Jinks*. —A little farther down is

The Royal Exchange, which was founded in 1753, and finished in 1761, at a cost of upwards of £31,000. It is built in the form of a square, with an open court in the centre, 86 feet by 96. The north side of the quadrangle contains the apartments of the Town Council, the Court-room of the Magistrates, and the various offices connected with the municipal affairs of the city, and with George Heriot's Hospital.—On the opposite side is

The Police Office, erected in 1849 in a plain Italian style, and having ample interior accommodation. Between the Police Office and St. Giles' Church stands the old "**Mercat Croce**" of Edinburgh, renowned in the annals of the city

ANCIENT CITY CROSS.

and of the kingdom, and not less in legendary story. It was here that James IV. and a long array of nobles were summoned to their doom by ghostly beings from the nether regions, and here, in the persecuting times many of the noblest of the land were done to death by knife or halter. Here, too, was the central point of royal pageants and loyal rejoicings, royal proclamations and legal distresses. The Cross was demolished in 1756, and the shaft removed to the grounds of Drum, near Gilmerton. It was brought back to the city a few years ago. In November, 1885, it was restored in its present handsome form by the Right Hon. W. E. Gladstone, M.P., from designs by Mr. Sidney Mitchell, who has made the new octagon tower as like as possible to that which existed at the time of Flodden. The inscription, translated from the Latin, is as follows :—This ancient monument, the Cross of Edinburgh, which of old was set apart for public ceremonies, but, having been utterly destroyed by a misguided hand, A.D. MDCCLVI., was avenged as well as lamented, in song alike noble and manful, by that great man Walter Scott, has now, by favour of the Magistrates of the city, been restored by William Ewart Gladstone, who claims, through both parents, a purely Scottish descent.

Adjoining, on the east, is the **Old Fishmarket Close**, formerly the residence of George Heriot and Lord President Dundas.—A little farther east is **Assembly Close**, where Lord President Dourie resided, and which contained the City Assembly Rooms from 1720 till 1726.—Opposite, on the left, is No. 243, **Anchor Close**, in a house at the bottom of which lived the mother of Drummond of Hawthornden, and George Drummond, Lord Provost of Edinburgh, who died in 1766. An old tavern here was the resort of the Crochallan Fencibles, celebrated by Burns.—On the right is No. 162, **Covenant Close**, in an old edifice in which the National Covenant was signed in 1638.—On the left is No. 221, **Stamp Office Close**, in which the Earls of Eglinton had their town mansion. It was afterwards converted into a tavern, which became a favourite resort of men of rank and fashion; and in which the Earl of Leven, for twenty years Lord High Commissioner to the General Assembly of the Church of Scotland, annually took up his abode, and held his levees. —A few yards farther east, in the third floor of an old land at the head of the **Fleshmarket Close** (No. 199), Henry Dundas, Viscount Melville, whose monument stands in St Andrew Square, resided for many years when he began to practise as an advocate.—Passing **Cockburn Street**, on the left, a thoroughfare constructed in 1859 to connect the Old Town with the Railway Termini, and **Hunter Square**, on the right, which stands on the site of Kennedy's Close, where George Buchanan died, we reach

The Tron Church, which was formerly called Christ's Church; but from its vicinity to the tron, or public weighing-beam, which once stood here, it obtained its present name. It was built in 1637-63, at a cost of nearly £6000. The original wooden spire having been burnt down in 1824, the present elegant stone steeple, 160 feet high, was erected in 1828.

On the opposite side is No. 177, now occupied as a shop, but which was formerly a cellar, in which the Commissioners appointed to sign the Articles of Union in 1707 secretly met and completed their signatures to that document, the enraged mob having driven them from their first meeting-place, Moray House.—A little farther down, entering by an archway, is No. 173, **Milne Square**, erected in 1689, as an Old Town improvement, and at one time the residence of a number of distinguished people. Charles Erskine of Tinwald, Lord Justice-Clerk in 1748, long resided in two flats of the large building on the west side of the Square, which now overlooks Cockburn Street; and here, too, on the 17th of October 1751, Robert Ferguson the poet was born.

Allan Ramsay's Shop.— Passing the North and South Bridges, we come to an old

ALLAN RAMSAY'S SHOP.

timber-fronted tenement, on the left, nearly opposite Niddry Street, in the first floor of a common stair in which, numbered 155, Allan Ramsay began business as a bookseller, and published many of his works. His dwelling-house was the floor immediately above.—A few paces farther east is No. 135,

Carrubber's Close, a place of some antiquarian interest. It contained the oldest Episcopal chapel in the city, which, till lately, was used as a place of worship by the body since the overthrow of Episcopacy in 1688. Captain Henderson, the antiquary, and Sir William Forbes of Pitsligo, whom Burns used frequently to visit, formerly resided here. And in an old building which formerly stood here, originally erected by Allan Ramsay as a theatre, but for more than half-a-century used as a church, Edward Irving, Dr M'Crie, the biographer of Knox, and other eminent men, frequently preached.—Adjoining is No. 129, **Bishop's Close**, which was at one time inhabited by Archbishop Spottiswood, Lady Jane Douglas, Sir James Montgomery, Lord Advocate for Scotland in 1777, and the first Lord President Dundas, and here his son, Henry Dundas, Viscount Melville, he of St Andrew Square, was born.—On the opposite side is No. 118, **Dickson's Close**, which formerly contained the town mansions of the Haliburton family and of Sir John Halliday of Tilybole, and the house of David Allan, "the Scottish Hogarth," as he was called. The tall building at the head of the close was also the residence of a number of persons of distinction, but is now chiefly occupied by **Buchanan's Temperance Hotel**.—Immediately adjoining, on the east, is No. 104,

Strichen's Close, which contains the town mansion of the Abbots of Melrose, the original gardens attached to which extended down to the Cowgate and up part of the opposite slope. The house was afterwards occupied by the well-known Sir George Mackenzie of Rosehaugh, Lord Advocate during the reigns of Charles II. and James II., and subsequently by a relative, Lord Strichen, whose name the close still bears.—A few paces farther east is

Blackfriar's Street, on the site of which, till lately, stood Blackfriar's Wynd, for more than 500 years one of the most aristocratic quarters of the Old Town—the abode of princes, cardinals, archbishops, bishops, and peers. But the buildings having fallen into decay, were recently taken down, and the present street formed. Here dwelt the Earls of Morton, the Lords Home, and the princely St Clair, Earl of Orkney, whose dame was attended by "seventy-five gentlewomen, whereof fifty-three were daughters of noblemen, all clothed in velvets and silks, with their chains of gold!" At the bottom of the Wynd, with a projecting turret to the Cowgate, stood the palace of Cardinal Beaton, Archbishop of Glasgow, where the Earl of Arran, attended by his kinsmen and friends, and the chief nobility of the west, assembled in 1542 to deliberate on his claim to the Regency of the kingdom, and where Queen Mary, with the chief nobles of her court, was entertained on the 9th of February 1561. Here, for many an age, prelatic pomp and princely pride held sway, and contending factions fought for mastery. It was down this way, during the famous "cleanse-the-causeway" contests, that the victorious adherents of the Earl of Angus rushed to assault the palace of the Cardinal-Archbishop, and wreak their vengeance on his person; and here, in 1588, the retainers of the haughty Earl of Bothwell and those of Sir William Stewart crossed swords in a bloody fray, when the latter was slain by a thrust from the sword of his rival. Up here, too, at eleven o'clock on the evening of the 10th of February 1567, her attendants bearing lighted torches before her, passed Queen Mary, on her way home to Holyrood Palace from her last visit to the unfortunate Darnley— just three hours before his murder. Here, also, at the head of the wynd, in 1668, the unfortunate Archbishop Sharpe of St Andrews—who was afterwards dragged from his carriage at Magus Moor, in Fife, in 1679, and slain by Hackston of Rathillet, and some others,—while seated in his coach waiting for the Bishop of Orkney, who resided here, was fired at by an assassin, who missed him, but dangerously wounded the bishop. Here, too, was situated one of the only two fashionable boarding-schools at one time in Edinburgh, the other being in the Canongate. And it was in the fashionable Episcopal Chapel, founded by Lord Chief-Baron Smith, that formerly stood here, that Dr Johnson, accompanied by Boswell and Sir William Forbes, attended divine service during his visit to Edinburgh, on Sunday the 15th of August 1773.

A little farther east stood **Toddrick's Wynd**, where the Danish ambassadors and nobles who accompanied Anne of Denmark, Queen of James VI., to this country in 1590 were entertained at a grand banquet by the magistrates. It was down this ancient alley, also, that the Earl of Bothwell and his followers passed on their way to murder Darnley on the night of the 10th of February 1567.—Almost opposite, on the left, is No. 101,

Paisley's Close, at the head of which some years ago there stood a tall fine old stone land, with the date 1612 carved on it, and in a shop in which Sir William Fettes, the founder of the magnificent hospital which bears his name, made the fortune which he left to rear it. A rather melancholy interest attaches to this place. Shortly after midnight, on Saturday the 10th of November 1861, the massive pile, that had stood for nearly 250 years, suddenly sank to the ground, and shot out into the broad way a heap of rubbish, burying twenty-three persons in the ruins. A few of the inmates almost miraculously escaped destruction from the peculiar way in which a portion of the material had fallen upon them, and amongst these was the lad whose sculptured effigy, as a memorial of this, now decorates the new building, with a scroll inscribed with the words he was heard uttering by those who were digging in the ruins for bodies—"Heave awa, chaps [lads], I'm no deid yet."

Chalmer's Close, a little farther down, on the same side (No. 81), was a favourite haunt of Lord Jeffrey in his boyhood, having been the residence of his grandfather. It also contained the mansion of John de Hope, the founder of the Hopetoun family, who came from France in 1537, in the retinue of the Princess Magdalene, the queen of James V.—Nearly opposite, on the right, is No. 56,

South Grey's Close, which contains the town mansion of the Earls of Selkirk and Stirling, now converted into the chapel house attached to St Patrick's Roman Catholic Chapel. This chapel, by the way, contains some fine altar paintings by Runciman. Near the foot of the close, on the left, is **Elphinstone's Court**, built by Sir James Elphinstone in 1679 ; and which was afterwards the residence of Sir Francis Scott of Thirlstane, Patrick Wedderburn (Lord Chesterhall), and Lord Stonefield. Here the celebrated Alexander Wedderburn, Lord Loughborough, and Lord High Chancellor of England, spent the first twenty years of his life. Fifty years afterwards, when he had retired from public life, and while on a visit to the city, he was taken in a chair, at his own earnest request, to the little court here where he had played when a boy, and on seeing in the ground some small holes which he had used while engaged in youthful games, he appeared to be deeply moved.—On the other side of the close, a few paces farther down, is the **Mint Court**, a sombre-looking quadrangle, formed of an irregular assemblage of buildings of various ages and styles, the oldest of which, a tall, massive, grim-looking, turreted building of polished ashlar, bears the date 1574, and was erected for the use of the National Mint. In this now squalid place was the lodging of the celebrated Earl of Argyll in 1675 ; and towards the close of the last century, a house on the north side was the residence of the eminent physician, Dr Cullen, while Lord Hailes occupied a more ancient one on the south. The west side of the court was at one time the abode of Lord Belhaven, Lord Haining, the Countess of Stair, Douglas of Cavers, and other eminent people.

Immediately adjoining this close, No. 50, is **Hyndford's Close**, containing, in a confined little court at the bottom, the ancient mansion of the Earls of Hyndford ; and which at a later period was occupied by Dr Rutherford, the maternal grandfather of Sir Walter Scott. This fine old house was afterwards a favourite haunt of Sir Walter's during his boyhood, and a very fine view of it from the garden behind is given in the Abbotsford edition of his works.—On the other side of the street, and projecting a little way into it, stands

John Knox's House, one of the oldest buildings in the city. (Open Wednesdays and Saturdays from 10 till 4. Admission, 6d. Apply at the shop below). Knox lived here in 1559, but before his occupancy it was the town residence of George Durie, the last Abbot of Dunfermline. Here the great Reformer wrote the most part, if not the whole, of his History of the Reformation ; here, too, he narrowly escaped the bullet of an assassin, which struck the candlestick before him while he was sitting in meditation ; and here, at 11 o'clock on the evening of the 24th of November 1572, he died, at the age of sixty-seven, " not so much oppressed with years, as worn out and exhausted by his extraordinary labour of body and anxiety of mind." Extending over nearly the entire front above the ground floor are inscribed in large Roman letters, "the first and great commandment, and the second which is like unto it :"—" LUFE . GOD . ABUFE AL . AND . VI . NYCHTBOUR . AS . YI . SELF." On an angle of the building, near a window from which the Reformer is said to have frequently addressed the populace, is a small effigy of Moses kneeling, and resting one hand on the Table of

JOHN KNOX'S HOUSE BEFORE THE ERECTION OF THE ADJOINING CHURCH.

the Law, while with the other he points to the name of God emblazoned above.

The place of worship adjoining belongs to the Free Church body, and is named after the Reformer. It is a modern Gothic edifice, highly ornate in character, and was erected in 1850. —The contracted part of the High Street, from John Knox's House to the Canongate, is called

The Nether Bow.—It derived its name from a massive battlemented structure with flanking towers and steeple, which stood for centuries as a gateway, extending from St Mary's Wynd to Leith Wynd. In this confined little spot was the residence of Sharpe, Archbishop of St Andrews ; of Thomas Bassendyne and Robert Lekprevik in 1570-74, two of our earliest Scottish printers ; and here William Falconer, the author of " The Shipwreck," was born.—A little below Knox's House, on the right, is No 16,

Tweeddale Court, at the bottom of which, in an enclosed court, stands the fine old town mansion of the noble family of Tweeddale, now occupied by the Messrs Oliver & Boyd, publishers. It is a building of the early part of the 17th century ; and the last family occupant was the fourth Marquis, who was Secretary of State for Scotland in 1742. It was afterwards occupied by the British Linen Banking Company ; and, in 1808, was the scene of one of the most mysterious murders that had ever taken place in the city. One evening about dusk, as one of the Bank porters, named Begbie, was entering the close, having in his possession upwards of £4000, which he was bringing from the Leith Branch, he was, when only a few paces from the busy public thoroughfare, suddenly stabbed to the heart with a knife, and robbed of the large sum he carried. And although a reward of 500 guineas was offered, no trace of the murderer could ever be obtained.

St Mary's Street, formerly St Mary's Wynd, on the right, before the formation of the South Bridge, was the main outlet to one of the great roads to the south, and the seat of several of the principal inns. It derived its name from an ancient Cistercian nunnery, which stood on its west side, dedicated to St Mary. All the old buildings that formerly stood on the east side have recently been swept away in the progress of city improvements ; and amongst these was the Old White Horse Inn, at which Dr Johnson put up on his arrival here in 1773.—On the opposite side is

Leith Wynd, anciently one of the principal outlets and avenues to the town, and the scene of many a lawless act and desperate fray. At the foot of this wynd, in open day, in February 1592, John Graham of Killearn, one of the supreme criminal judges, was waylaid and murdered, and not one of the perpetrators was ever brought to justice. Down this steep incline, too, clattered Graham of Claverhouse and thirty of his dragoons, when on his way to raise the Highland clans in favour of King James, while the town was beating to arms to pursue him. This wynd has now been removed to make way for a new street, to be named after Lord Jeffrey.

THE CANONGATE

extends from the Nether Bow to Holyrood, and, like the High Street and the Lawnmarket, was anciently the abode of the noble and wealthy. Here dwelt the Dukes of Hamilton and Queensberry, the Countesses of Tweeddale and Lothian ; the Earls of Breadalbane, Hyndford, Haddington, Dalhousie, Panmure, Moray, and Mar, and a host of others equally distinguished. "As the main avenue from the palace to the city," says Chambers, "it has borne upon its pavement the burden of all that was beautiful, all that was gallant, all that has become historically interesting in Scotland for the last six or seven hundred years." Up here, too, marched the death procession of Montrose, "the hero seated on a hurdle, with beard untrimmed, hair dishevelled, dragged through the crowded street by the city hangman and his horses, yet proud of aspect, and flashing on his enemies on the balcony above him the fires of his disdain." (*See notice of Moray House, page* 38.) And although age and the exigencies of modern sanitary requirements have wrought sad havoc amongst the old houses that formerly stood here, there still remain not a few to which belong historical and literary associations of the most interesting kind. Scott, who loved every locality of the Old Town, delighted to linger here. "No funeral hearse," says Lockhart, "crept more leisurely than did his landau up the Canongate ; and not a queer tottering gable but recalled to him some long-buried memory of splendour or bloodshed, which, by a few words, he set before the hearer in the reality of life." Part of this old street was built as early as the twelfth century, and many of the existing houses date as far back as the sixteenth ; one bears the date 1565.

The first place of note on the left is the Morocco Land, No. 285, an interesting old edifice with an antique gabled façade to the street, adorned with the figure of a turbaned Moor occupying a pulpit, and regarding which various romantic stories are told, one of which is, that a young citizen of Edinburgh, having been condemned to death for some riotous proceedings, escaped from prison the night before the day appointed for his execution, took ship at Leith, and fled abroad. But having been captured by pirates, and sold as a slave, he won the favour of the Emperor of Morocco, by whom he was promoted to rank and wealth. Having returned to his native city at a period when the plague was raging, and the provost's only daughter lay at the point of death, he intimated his possession of an elixir of wondrous potency, and undertook to cure her, and did. The result is soon told. He married her, and settled down in this house as a wealthy citizen of the Canongate ; and in gratitude to his royal patron, adorned the front of his residence with the effigy of his Moorish majesty.—A little farther down, on the same side, is New Street, whose last century occupants were Lord Kames—his house is at the head of the street, on the east side ; Lord Hailes, Sir Philip Ainslie, Lady Anstruther, Dr Young, a celebrated physician of the period ; Miss Jean Ramsay, a daughter of the poet, &c.—Almost opposite is the Playhouse Close, No. 196, in which, in 1746, the first theatre in Edinburgh was erected, and where, on the evening of the 14th of December 1746, Home's tragedy of "Douglas" was first presented to the public. St John's Cross.—A few paces to the east, a ringed spot on the causeway indicates where St John's Cross, the ancient eastern boundary of the capital, formerly stood, and where Charles I., at his ceremonial entry into Edinburgh in 1633, knighted the provost. The shaft of this old cross is still to be seen fixed to the wall at the Canongate Tolbooth.—A little farther down, on the same side, entering through an archway, is

St John Street, an aristocratic quarter of the last century, begun in 1768. In a house at the head of the street, facing the Canongate, the Earl of Hopetoun resided in 1788 ; and in the first floor of the same building on the west side of the street, Smollett, the novelist, resided in 1766, with his sister, Mrs Telfer of Scotstown. No. 13, on the east side of the street, was the residence of Lord Monboddo, and his lovely and accomplished daughter, Miss Burnet, who died prematurely of consumption on the 17th of June 1790, and whom Burns, who was a frequent guest of her father's, describes so glowingly in his "Address to Edinburgh,"—

"Fair Burnet strikes the adoring eye,
   Heaven's beauties on my fancy shine ;
I see the Sire of Love on high,
   And own His work indeed divine !"

and whose early death he has so touchingly commemorated in a special ode. No. 10, on the same side, was the residence of James Ballantyne, Scott's confidential critic and partner; and here those select dinners took place that Ballantyne was in the habit of giving occasionally to his choice literary allies and personal friends, that he might read to them a chapter or two from some forthcoming romance of Scott's. Scott himself, Lockhart, who so graphically describes the scenes, Erskine, Terry, Sir William Allan, George Hogarth, W.S., Mrs Ballantyne's brother, and the author of a history of music, &c., were frequent guests. Sir David Rae, Lord Justice-Clerk in 1799, also resided in a house on the east side here. The first house on the west side, a few paces south of the archway, was the meeting place of the Canongate Kilwinning Lodge of Free Masons, where Burns was made a member and poet-laureate of the lodge. A house a little to the south of this, with its gable to the street, and a garden to the south, was the residence, in 1780, of the Earl of Wemyss.—Exactly opposite St John Street there is a large and lofty stone building which has had for occupants the Countess of Eglinton, David Hume, who wrote most part of his history here, and others of like note.— To the east of this, on the opposite side, is

MORAY HOUSE.

Moray House, a large and conspicuous edifice, originally erected by the Countess of Home in 1628, from whom it passed in 1645, to the noble house of Moray, whose town mansion and property it remained for two hundred years. Oliver Cromwell took up his residence here, on his first visit to Edinburgh, in the summer of 1648, and again in the winter of 1650, after the victory of Dunbar, and held his levees in the principal rooms. On the 13th of May 1650, the mansion was the scene of much festivity and rejoicing on the occasion of the marriage of the Earl of Moray's eldest daughter, Lady Mary Stuart, to Lord Lorn, afterwards better known as the unfortunate Earl of Argyll. The day of the marriage happened to be the day on which the great Marquis of Montrose was dragged a prisoner up the Canongate upon the hangman's hurdle, and the wedding guests, including the Earl of Loudon, then Lord Chancellor of the kingdom, Lord Warriston, and the Countess of Haddington, along with the Marquis of Argyll and the bride and bridegroom, so far forgot their dignity as to step out on the old stone balcony that overhangs the street, to gaze on the degradation of their fallen enemy. Two days afterwards Montrose perished on the scaffold; but, ere many years had elapsed three of those onlookers, including the gay and happy bridegroom, had perished by the hands of the common executioner, on the same fatal spot to which the brave but unfortunate Montrose was passing. In 1707, when the house was in the temporary occupancy of Lord Chancellor Seafield, many confidential deliberations, in connection with the Treaty of Union, took place within its walls; and it was in a little summer-house which formerly adorned the stately old terraced gardens behind that the Commissioners met to sign the Articles, when the violence of the enraged mob compelled them to desist. The subscription was afterwards completed in a cellar, now a newsvender's shop, No. 177 High Street. After having been occupied for some time by the British Linen Company's Bank, this old residence was, in 1847, transformed into the Free Church Normal School, and the fine garden became the playground of children.—A few paces farther east, on the left, is

The Canongate Tolbooth, which formed the court-house and jail of the burgh, and is regarded as a good example of Scottish architecture of the time of James VI. It is surmounted by a tower and spire, flanked by two turrets in front, from between which a large clock projects into the street. The building is adorned with a variety of mottoes and sculptured devices which prevailed at the period of its erection. Under one of the windows, a carved tablet bears the following inscription—"PATRIE ET POSTERIS, 1591." Over the inner doorway, which leads both to the court-house and the prison, are the strikingly appropriate words, "ESTO FIDUS!"

CANONGATE TOLBOOTH.

A portion of the street flat is now used as a police station, over the door of which is placed the burgh armorial bearing—a stag's head and horns—with the motto—"SIC ITUR AD ASTRA" —a strange way indeed to the stars! By the side of the wall, eastward of the entrance to the police station, is the shaft of the ancient market cross, which formerly stood in the centre of the roadway.—A few steps farther eastward brings us to

The Canongate Church, erected in 1688, from funds bequeathed by one Thomas Moodie in 1649. It is a plain-looking structure with a painted front, surmounted by an ornamental model of a stag's head, the burgh crest. The well-known Dr Hugh Blair, and the late Principal Lee, were at one time parish ministers here. In the surrounding graveyard lie the remains of

FERGUSON'S TOMB.

Ferguson, the poet, whose tombstone, raised at the expense of Robert Burns, "to remain for ever sacred to the memory of him whose name it bears, and who was born September 5, 1751, died October 16, 1774"—contains the following verse—

"No sculptured marble here, nor pompous lay,
No storied urn, nor animated bust—
This simple stone directs pale Scotia's way
To pour her sorrows o'er her Poet's dust;

Dr Adam Ferguson, historian of the Roman Republic; Dugald Stewart, Professor of Moral Philosophy; Adam Smith, the well-known author of the "Wealth of Nations;" David Allan, the artist; Dr Burney, the author of the History of Music, &c.

A little farther down, on the same side, is No. 129, **Panmure Close**, which gave access to Panmure House, the residence of the Earls of Panmure. Here also Adam Smith resided for the last twelve years of his life.—On the opposite side, within an enclosure, is No. 90, **Milton House**, built and occupied as a town mansion by Andrew Fletcher of Milton, Lord Justice-Clerk of Scotland in 1724.—Farther down, on the right, is

Queensberry House, a huge ungainly pile, with centre and projecting wings, built in the time of Charles II. by the first Duke of Queensberry, the time-serving and unprincipled minister of the last two Stuarts. The most distinguished occupant of the house latterly.

however, was the wife of the third Duke, the beautiful and accomplished Lady Catherine Hyde, the patroness of the poet Gay, and whose sprightliness and wit have been sung in the poetry of Pope, Swift, and Prior. Gay, who accompanied the Duke and Duchess to Scotland in 1729, resided here for a short time; and tradition points out an old house on the opposite side, which was formerly an alehouse, kept by

JENNY HA'S.

one Janet Hall,—*Jenny Ha's*, as it was called—where the poet is said to have spent many jovial hours in the company of Allan Ramsay and a few other choice spirits of the city. William, third Earl of March and fourth Duke of Queensberry, was the last member of the family who occupied the house. Having grown dissatisfied with it, he caused it to be stripped of all its ornaments and sold. With about sixty-five rooms, and a gallery seventy feet long, it was offered for £900.

The Government of the day purchased it for a barrack; but it is now used as a House of Refuge for the Destitute.

On the left, entered by Galloway's Entry, is **Whiteford House**, built by Sir John Whiteford, and latterly occupied by Lord Bannatyne, who died here in 1823. A little farther down is No 31, **Whitehorse Close**, which contains the Whitehorse Inn, an ancient hostelry erected in 1623, and which Scott, in "Waverley," makes the resort of the officers of Prince Charles Edward's army, and the quarters of Captain Waverley.—Proceeding eastwards, towards Holyrood, we reach a radiated arrangement of the causeway, which marks the site of the Girth Cross, the ancient boundary of the **Abbey Sanctuary**—the only remaining place of the kind in Scotland. An *imperium in imperio*, it has its own courts, and judges, and laws, and can protect its subjects from all the bailiffs in the kingdom. Along the wall of the Abbey Court-house, on the right, will be observed a series of pointed arches that have been built up. These indicate the ancient Gothic porch and gatehouse which led into the Abbey Close. On the west side of the Palace Yard is the royal mews and guardhouse.

The Fountain.—The beautiful fountain in front of the Palace was erected in 1859, at a cost of £1700. This elaborately carved structure was designed by Mr Matheson, of H.M. Board of Works, after a model of the fountain that anciently adorned the quadrangle of Linlithgow Palace. Octagonal at the base, which is surrounded by a circular basin, it is divided into three stages in the height, the first being enclosed by a beautifully-cut rail, with floreated pinnacles, and figures of animals at the alternate angles, the second having figures of musicians, &c., while the third is surmounted by an imperial crown, supported by four yeomen of the guard. The crown forms a cistern from which the water falls into the lower basin, and is then expelled from the lions' heads into the basin at the bottom. The figures and heads are principally representations of historical characters, some of whom were associated with Holyrood.

ANCIENT DOORWAY, BLACKFRIAR'S WYND.

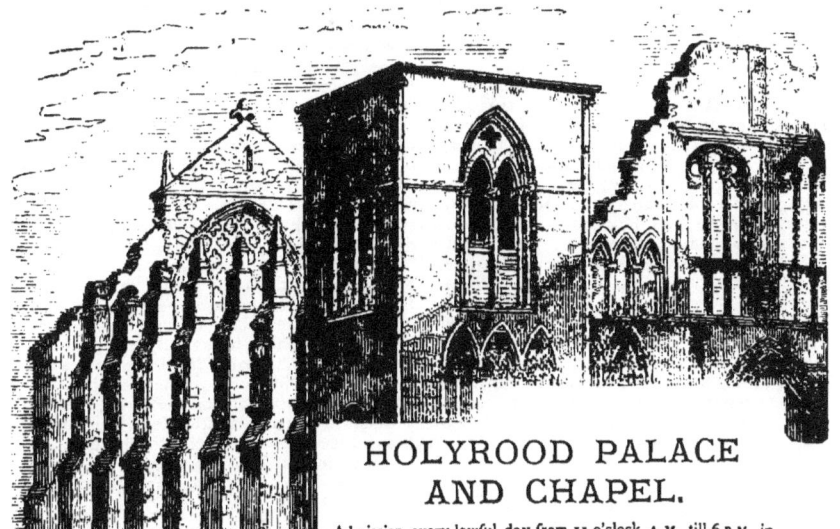

HOLYROOD PALACE AND CHAPEL.

Admission every lawful day from 11 o'clock A.M. till 6 P.M. in summer, and from 11 A.M. till 4 P.M. in winter. A charge of sixpence is made—except on Saturday, which is a *free day*.

We now enter the precincts of a place in which centre many of the most interesting historical associations of the kingdom—

"A deserted palace, where no monarch dwells!"

The Palace.—The Palace of Holyrood House was distinct from the Abbey or Monastery, and was founded by James IV. in 1501. The building, however, made little progress during his reign. In 1528 James V. erected the north-west towers, where Queen Mary's apartments are

JAMES THE FIFTH'S TOWERS.

situated. The rest of the existing Palace was built by command of Charles II. in 1671-1679, after a design furnished by Sir William Bruce of Kinross, and which is said to have been a copy of the Château de Chantilly in France, the residence of the famous Condé family. The Palace as it now stands is a spacious and imposing quadrangular structure, in what is called the Palladian style, enclosing a piazza-bounded court 94 feet square. The principal front faces the west, and consists of a double battlemented tower on each side, which are connected by a receding screen or range of building two stories high. In the centre of this front is the grand entrance, which is decorated on each side with four Doric columns, above which are sculptured the royal arms of Scotland, beneath an open pediment, surmounted by a small octagonal tower terminating in an imperial crown. The other sides of the quadrangle are three stories high. Since the union of the two kingdoms, the Palace has occasionally been occupied by Charles I., Charles II., James VII., Prince Charles Edward, the Duke of Cumberland, George IV., and the present royal family. From 1795-1799 a suite of apartments in the eastern side of the quadrangle was occupied by the exiled royal family of France; in 1830-33, Charles X., again an exile, occupied the same apartments.

The Picture Gallery.—On entering the Palace by the front gateway, turning to the left and ascending the stair, the first door reached is that leading to the Picture Gallery. This fine apartment, measuring 150 feet in length, 24 feet in breadth, and about 20 feet in height, is a portion of the additions made to the Palace in Charles the Second's time. On its walls are hung a hundred imaginary portraits of both fabulous and reputed kings of Scotland, all painted in 1684-86 by a Flemish artist named De Witt. Many of these paintings were cut and slashed by

General Hawley's cowardly dragoons after their defeat at Falkirk, but were subsequently repaired. At the east end of the Gallery are four pictures of some little historic, antiquarian, and artistic value. One (46*) represents James III. and his son James IV.—on the reverse, the Holy Trinity; the other (47*), Margaret of Denmark, queen of James III.—on the reverse, Sir Edward Boncle, Provost of Trinity College Church. They are supposed to have been painted as an altar-piece for the Church of the Holy Trinity by an artist of the Van Eck school, about 1484. The figure seated at the organ in the character of St Cecilia represents Queen Mary of Gueldres, by whom the church was founded in 1462, accompanied by one of her daughters, and the Provost, as her confessor, offering up his devotions to the Holy Trinity. These two paintings were long in the Royal Collection at Hampton Court, having been carried thither at the Union, but were restored to Scotland in 1857. In this magnificent apartment Prince Charles Edward Stuart held his receptions and balls in 1745. It is now only used for the election of the Scottish representative Peers, and for the annual levees of the Lord High Commissioner to the General Assembly of the Church of Scotland.

Lord Darnley's Rooms.—On leaving the Picture Gallery, the next rooms visited are those which Lord Darnley used to occupy, in which are a number of interesting portraits, amongst which is one of the youthful Darnley himself and his brother, numbered 132, and some fine specimens of ancient tapestry. From these the visitor ascends the staircase to

Queen Mary's Apartments, which are on the third floor of James V.'s towers, and form the most interesting portion of the palace buildings—that portion where the loveliest woman of her age—whom no man ever beheld without admiration, and whose history none can read without sorrow—spent the most eventful years of her chequered and unhappy life.

The Audience-Chamber. — The first apartment entered is the audience-chamber, a room 24 feet by 22, with the roof divided into panelled compartments embellished with the initials and armorial bearings of royal personages, and the walls of which are hung with ancient tapestry. Here, amongst other articles of furniture, there are some richly-embroidered chairs, and a venerable state bed, said to have been used by Charles I. while resident in Holyrood; by Prince Charles Edward, before and after the battle of Prestonpans, in September 1745; and by the Duke of Cumberland, on the evening of the 30th January 1746, before setting out for Culloden, and after his return from it, in the spring of the same year. In this apartment also, the stern old Reformer had frequent stormy interviews with its beautiful but unfortunate occupant. In one of the very last he had, in May 1563, a strikingly characteristic scene occurred here. Knox, having been summoned to answer before the Queen for some remarks he had made in reference to her marriage with Darnley, was brought, after dinner, into her private cabinet by Erskine of Dun. After a brief interview, in which the Reformer mildly defended himself, but in doing so gave utterance to some rather uncourtly truths, Mary, in a passionate outburst of tears, commanded him to leave the apartment. In doing so, the Reformer, passing into the outer or audience-chamber, found himself shunned and avoided by the nobles of the court who waited here. He was not, however, a man to be cast down by the desertion of such summer friends as these. Observing a number of the ladies of the queen's household sitting near, in their gorgeous apparel, he approached them, and, in a speech in the very vein of Hamlet, said, between jest and earnest—"Ah, fair ladies, how pleasant were this life of yours, if it should ever abide, and then in the end we might pass to heaven with this gear! But fie on that knave, Death—that will come whether ye will or no; and when he hath laid on the arrest, then foul worms will be busy with this flesh, be it never so fair and tender; and the silly soul, I fear, shall be so feeble, that it can carry with it neither gold, garnishing, pearl, nor precious stones!" And having said this, he departed.

The Bed-Chamber.—The next apartment to this is the bed-chamber, 22 feet by 18 feet, and the roof of which is divided into panels adorned with various initials and coats of arms. Here are shown the queen's bed, the moth-eaten and decayed hangings of which are of crimson damask, with green silk fringes and tassels; some pieces of tapestry, illustrative of the classical

QUEEN MARY.

story of the fall of Phæton; and portraits of Queen Mary herself, Henry VIII., and Queen Elizabeth.

The Dressing-Room.—At the south-west corner of this chamber a narrow door leads to the dressing-room, a small place, some ten feet square, hung with faded tapestry.

Private Staircase and Supper-Room. —On the north side is a small door which opens on the private staircase by which the assassins of Rizzio ascended to the royal apartments; and close to this door is the entrance to the supper-room,* or rather closet, where, on the night of the

* Dr Johnson, accompanied by Boswell and Principal Robertson, the historian, visited these apartments while

9th of March 1566, the unfortunate Rizzio was dragged from behind the person of the queen, to whose garments he had clung for protection, and after being hustled through the bedroom and antechamber, during which he received nearly fifty wounds, was finally despatched at the head of the staircase by the daggers of the Earl of Morton, Lord Ruthven, Lord Lindsay, the Master of Ruthven, and "divers other gentlemen." Some dark stains, said to have been made by the blood of the ill-starred Italian, are still pointed out at the head of the stair.

QUEEN MARY'S BEDROOM.

Descending to the piazza of the inner court, and proceeding eastward, we reach the ruins of

The Chapel Royal, the only portion now remaining of the ancient Abbey of Holyrood, founded by King David I. in 1128. Dilapidated by Edward II. in 1322, burned by Richard II. in 1385, restored by Abbot Crawford about the end of the 15th century, again sacked by the English in 1547, when the transepts and choir were destroyed, stripped of its ecclesiastical adornments at the Reformation, and rifled by the mob in 1688, the portion now standing consists of the remains of the nave of the ancient building, originally 148 feet long and 66 feet broad, and a wall built by the first reformers across its east end, to convert it into a parish church. In the interior of the chapel, the two shattered piers at the north-east end are all that remain of the seven that originally divided the nave from the aisles. The great east window, 34 feet high by 20 feet broad, is of comparatively modern origin, and was blown out in a violent storm, in 1795, but was restored in 1816 from its own remains, which lay scattered about on the ground. The most ancient portion of the present edifice is a small Norman doorway, now built up, at the back of the mass of masonry above the royal vault, and which origin-

GREAT EAST WINDOW OF CHAPEL ROYAL.

ally communicated with the old cloisters of the Abbey. It cannot be of later date than 1150. Almost all the west front, with its great tower and richly-ornamented doorway, is part of the original edifice, and is a beautiful specimen of the mixed

in Edinburgh, on the afternoon of Sunday the 15th of August 1773, and seems to have been touched with the desolate appearance they presented. While in the small supper-room, he was overheard repeating, in a muttering tone, a line of the beautiful old ballad, "Johnny Armstrong's Last Good-Night"—

And ran him through the fair bodie."

Norman and early English which prevailed in Scotland about 1170. The windows over the great doorway, however, and the ornamental

WEST FRONT AND GREAT DOORWAY OF CHAPEL ROYAL.

tablet between them, are additions of the time of Charles I., whose initials are below. The inscription which this unfortunate monarch caused to be carved on this tablet is a striking illustration of the instability of human hopes—"HE SHALL BUILD ANE HOUSE FOR MY NAME, AND I WILL STABLISH THE THRONE OF HIS KINGDOM FOR EVER." How this has been fulfilled, every reader of English history knows. A great portion of the north and south aisles is paved with flat grave-stones, a prevalent kind of sepulchral memorial during the fourteenth and fifteenth centuries. The oldest legible date on one of these is 1455. In this old chapel Charles I. was crowned, and James II., James III., and James IV., and Queen Mary and Darnley were married ; and here, in the royal vault at the south-east end, lie the remains of David II., James II., Mary of Gueldres, James V., the queen and second son of James V., the Duke of Albany, Lord Darnley, and many others of lesser note. In the north-west tower is the tomb of Lord Viscount Belhaven, councillor to Charles I., and one of the most remarkable men of his day, who died at Edinburgh on the 12th of January 1639, in the 63d year of his age. The monument, or rather altar tomb, is of Italian marble, and consists of a recumbent figure of the old nobleman in his robes of state with his coronet on his head, his right arm resting on a cushion, his head slightly raised, and his left arm supporting a sword. Fluted columns on either side of the figure support an open pediment, over which is the deceased's arms.

Leaving the palace, and turning southward, we enter

The Queen's Park, and pass in an easterly direction along the Queen's Drive. Nearly opposite the southern entrance gate of the Palace is St Margaret's Well, a small octagonal Gothic building of great antiquity, with a groined roof supported in the centre by a decorated pillar from which the water flows through grotesque gurgoils. It formerly stood on the old cross road leading from the Abbey Hill to the village of Restalrig ; and was anciently, from the supposed miraculous healing virtues of its waters, the resort of numerous pilgrims. As the railway works at St Margaret's threatened to destroy it, it was removed some years ago to its present site. Continuing our progress along the Drive, we catch a glimpse of the ruins of St Anthony's Chapel perched on the rising ground to the right. This chapel was a hermitage of the Carmelite Friars, attached to the preceptory of St Anthony, Leith. It is said to have originally been a beautiful Gothic structure well suited to the romantic spot on which it stands. A little below the chapel is St Anthony's Well, a spring of clear water that flows from the rock into a hollow stone basin, and then ripples through the long grass into the lake below, and which is celebrated in the plaintive old ballad, "O waly, waly, up yon bank." A small artificial sheet of water, called St Margaret's Loch, lies at the base of the hill on which the chapel stands. Passing this, the drive ascends the Whinny Hill, bringing into view Piershill Barracks, Portobello, and the Firth of Forth. At the bend of the road Dunsappie Loch meets the eye, on the slopes to the east of which the army of Prince Charles Edward encamped both before and after the battle of Prestonpans. Arthur Seat. — Should the visitor be desirous of reaching the top of Arthur's Seat, he may begin the ascent more easily from this point, as the hill is less abrupt here than on any of its other sides. It is 822 feet above the level of the sea, and the magnificent panoramic view to be had from the summit will well repay the labour of the ascent.—From the elevated position where we now are, we overlook the picturesque village of Duddingston, with its loch and swans, and its quaint old Saxon Church, in which Thomson the landscape-painter used to preach, and see, embosomed amid the trees on the rising ground beyond, the ruins of Craigmillar Castle, where Queen Mary often resided. The Drive now leads through a deep cutting in the rock, but ere long a fine view of country southward and westward opens before us. The suburb of Newington, with its villas and gardens, occupies the foreground, while the vista beyond is bounded by the hills of Blackford and Braid, and by the range of the Pentlands. The carriage road now descends a valley, and winds round the base of Salisbury Crags ; but the higher road, on the right, a pathway cut in the face of the Crags—the highest elevation of which is the central cavity of the Cat Nick, about 570 feet above the level of the sea—is the one most frequently taken, as its elevated platform affords a series of magnificent panoramic views of Edinburgh, the Firth of Forth, and the coast of Fife. It was a favourite walk of David Hume the historian, and of Sir Walter Scott, who says, "it used to be my favourite evening and morning resort, when engaged with a favourite author or new subject of study." Descending to the Palace Yard, and crossing to the North, we enter the Abbey Hill, passing, on the right, within the lawn enclosure, a curious old horologe called **Queen Mary's Dial**, but which was not erected till the time of Charles I., and on the left **Queen Mary's Bath**, a quaint, ancient octagonal tower.

Ascending Abbey Mount, and proceeding along the Regent Road, the first noticeable object, on the left, is

Burns's Monument, erected by subscription in 1830, after a design by Thomas Hamilton, the architect of the High School. The cupola of this elegant memorial is a copy of the monument of Lysicrates at Athens. The interior is tastefully fitted up as a museum, and contains a handsome bust of the poet by W. Brodie, R.S.A., and a number of interesting relics, which may be inspected daily from 10 till 4 on payment of 2d.—On the right, a little farther on, is

THE HIGH SCHOOL.

The date of the foundation of the High School is unknown, but it is ascertained to have existed as early as the beginning of the twelfth century. From that time to the Reformation, the "Grammar School of Edinburgh," as it was then called, was under the control of the Abbot or Commendator and Canons of Holyrood. In 1598, through the enlightened zeal of the clergy and Town Council, it was remodelled on a more comprehensive plan; and, from the special patronage vouchsafed to it by James VI., it received the name which it still bears, *Schola Regia Edimburgensis*. After the High School had been disjoined from the Abbey of Holyrood, a building was erected in 1578, to receive the pupils, in the gardens of the monastery of the Blackfriars, at the east end of Infirmary Street, near the head of the High School Wynd; but having fallen into decay, and being found otherwise unsuitable, it was, in 1777, replaced by another building, which continued to be used till 1829, when the present edifice was erected on the southern slope of the Calton Hill. Designed by Mr Thomas Hamilton, a pupil of the school, it was founded on the 28th of July 1825, and completed in June 1829, at a cost of £30,000. It is a structure of the purest Grecian Doric, on the plan of the celebrated Temple of Theseus at Athens, the main building consisting of a centre and two wings, having a total frontage of 270 feet. Two lofty corridors, each supported by six Doric columns, connect the centre with the wings. The centre contains the Rector's apartments, a spacious examination hall, 75 feet by 43, a library, hall, and one or two smaller rooms; the wings contain the Class-rooms for the two Classical Masters, and for their colleagues in other departments. The spacious playground, a portion of which is roofed over, extends to nearly two acres, and commands a beautiful and picturesque view of the ancient city and the surrounding country. The governing and instructing staff consists of a Rector, two Classical and two English Masters; Masters for French, German, Hindustani, Mathematics and Arithmetic, Writing and Bookkeeping, Engineering, Drawing, Fencing, Gymnastics; and Lecturers on Chemistry, Natural Philosophy, Zoology, and Botany, all appointed by the School Board, in whom the management of the school is vested. The curriculum extends over six years, and embraces every branch of knowledge now recognised as requisite for a liberal education. The High School of Edinburgh is one of the first educational institutions in the country. It has had for rectors and masters a series of the most eminent men that ever adorned the academic office; and, during the last six hundred years, it has exercised over the youth of Scotland an influence that has made itself felt wherever the English language is spoken. Perhaps no educational institution in the country has sent forth so many eminent men, in every department of literature, science, and art, as the following list of a few among the more distinguished of its pupils will shew :—

I. Divinity.—Dr Hugh Blair, George Hamilton, D.D., Gladsmuir; John Erskine, D.D, Edinburgh, author of "Theological Dissertations;" Greville Ewing (Independent Church, Glasgow), author of "Greek and English Scripture Lexicon;" Robert Haldane, author of "Commentary on the Romans;" Thomas Macknight, D.D., of Greyfriars' Church; the Rev Alexander Brunton. D.D., Professor of Oriental Languages, Edinburgh; the Rev. D. Welsh, D.D., Professor of Ecclesiastical History, Edinburgh; Dr Thomas M'Crie, Professor of Divinity in English Presbyterian Church; the Rev. Dr Paul, Edinburgh; the Rev. Dr Glover, Edinburgh the Rev R M. M'Cheyne, of Dundee, the Rev Charles Watson, D.D., Burntisland; Archibald C. Tait, Archbishop of Canterbury; John Strain, R. C. Bishop of Edinburgh; Dr Crawford, Professor of Divinity, Edinburgh; Dr Menzies of Hoddam, translator of Tholuck's "Commentaries;" Professor Goold, editor of Owen's Works, &c.; Dr Milligan, Professor of Church History, Aberdeen; Dr Wallace of Greyfriars'; the Rev. Alex Leitch, author of "Ethics of Theism," &c.

II. Law.—1 Lords High Chancellors of Great Britain—Erskine, Loughborough, Brougham; 2. Vice-Chancellor Sir John Stewart. 3. Judges and Advocates—Sir Cresswell Cresswell, Judge in the Divorce Court; Lord Dreghorn, Lord Woodhouselee, Lord Bannatyne, Lord Chief Commissioner Adam, William Alexander, Lord Chief Baron of England; Professor George Joseph Bell, author of "Treatise on the Law of Scotland;" Robert Bell, Lecturer on Conveyancing, and author of "Forms of Deeds;" Lord President Blair, Lord Succoth, Lord President Hope, Lord Justice-Clerk Hope, Lord Craigie, Lord Chief Baron Dundas of Arniston, Lord Clerk Register Dundas, Lord Reston, Lord Hermand, Lord Kinnedder, Baron Hume, author of "Criminal Law of Scotland;" Judge Advocate Gilbert Hutcheson, author of "Justice of Peace;" Lord Newton, Lord Glenlee, the Lords Meadowbank (father and son); Sir James Montgomery, Lord Advocate; Lord Cringletie, Sir William Rae, Lord Advocate Lord William Robertson (son of the historian); Lord Mackenzie, Lord Medwyn, Lord Moncreiff, Lord Murray, Lord Wood, Lord Pitmilly, Lord Patrick Robertson, Lord Dundrennan, Jeffrey, F Horner, Cockburn, Rutherford, Neaves Lord President Inglis, Lord Justice-Clerk Moncreiff, Lord Ardmillan, Lord Barcaple, James Anderson, Q.C., Walter Ross, author of "Lectures on Conveyancing;" John Watson, founder of "John Watson's Hospital;" Alexander Wight, author of "Treatise on the Laws of Election," John Wild, Professor of Civil Law, Edinburgh; Lord Balgray, Lord Adam Anderson, Sydney Bell, editor of "Law Reports of House of Lords" William Blair of Avontown, Judge in Ionian Islands, and author of a treatise on "Slavery among the Romans," Sir James Gibson-Craig. Bart. Sir William Gibson-Craig, Bart., Lord Clerk Register; Sir David Dundas, Solicitor-General for England, William Pitt Dundas, Deputy Clerk Register for Scotland Professor Douglas Chenpe; Professor Allan Menzies; Professor Cosmo Innes, the celebrated antiquary Henry Glassford Bell, Sheriff of Lanarkshire, author of "Life of Mary Queen of Scots," &c.; Sheriff Mark Napier, author of "Memoirs of Napier of Merchiston," "Marquis of Montrose," &c.; David Milne, author of "Essay on Comets" Robert Pitcairn, author of "Criminal Trials of Scotland;" James Reddie, author of "Historical View of the Law of Maritime Commerce;" Professor George Skene, Edinburgh.

III. Medicine.—The three Monros, and Robert Knox, anatomists — Professor Sir Charles Bell, author of "Bridgewater Treatise on the Hand;" John Bell, author of "Treatise on Gunshot Wounds;" Dr John Cheyne, author of "Essay on Mental Derangement;" Dr Andrew Combe, Physiologist; Dr Cruickshanks, author of "Treatise on Anatomy," Professor Andrew Duncan, Edinburgh; Professor James Russell, Edinburgh; Sir A W Crichton, Physician to the Emperor of Russia; Professor Fyfe, Aberdeen; Professor R. E. Grant, University College, London; Dr D. B. Reid, author of "Elements of Chemistry;" Sir William Ferguson, Professors Hope, Christison, Syme, Henderson, Maclagan, Crum Brown (Edinburgh), Young (Glasgow), Inglis (Aberdeen).

IV. Literature, Science, and Art.—William Drummond of Hawthornden, poet; Robert Blair, author of "The Grave," Robert Ferguson, poet; Professor Keill, Oxford; John Law of Lauriston, author of the "Mississippi Scheme;" James Boswell, biographer of Dr Johnson; Professor Bruce, Edinburgh; Professor Dugald Stewart, Dr Gilbert Stewart, Henry Mackenzie, "The Man of Feeling;" Professor Gilchrist of Calcutta; Professor Hamilton, Aberdeen; Sir Walter Scott, Sir John Sinclair of Ulbster; William Tytler of Woodhouselee, author of "Inquiry Regarding Mary Queen of Scots;" Patrick Fraser Tytler, author of "History of Scotland." George Combe, phrenologist; Sir G. S. Mackenzie of Coul, author of "Travels in Iceland;" A. N Carmichael, author of Treatise on "Greek Verb," &c.; William Smellie, author of "Philosophy of Natural History;" George Borrow, author of "Bible in Spain," &c.; John Thomson, first professor of music, University of Edinburgh J. B. Paterson, author of "Essay on National Character of the Athenians:" James Douglas of Cavers, essayist: Alex. Dyce, literary biographer, antiquary, and critic: Professors Pillans. George Wilson, author of the "Five Gateways of Knowledge;" Balfour, Macdougall, Calderwood, Edinburgh; Professors Walker, Sir D. K. Sandford, Ramsay, Arnot, Glasgow; Dr W. M. Gunn, editor of Livy, Virgil, &c., and author of "Lectures on National Education," &c. Professor Daniel Wilson Toronto, author of "Pre-Historic Annals of Scotland;" Alexander Colston, author of essays on "Basis of Moral Science;" James D. Burns, author of "The Vision of Prophecy, and other Poems;" Professor Sanders, Calcutta; the Rev. A. L. Simpson, art-critic and lecturer; Colonel Alfred B. Richards, promoter of the volunteer movement in England, and author of various plays and poems. Leonard Horner, president of Geological Society; Professor Gordon, Glasgow; A Keith Johnston, F.R.G.S., geographer in ordinary to Her Majesty; Allan Stevenson, engineer, Professor Williamson, Canada; Nasmyth, inventor of "Steam Hammer;" Robert Adam, architect. Robert and William Mylne, architects; Thomas Hamilton, architect of High School; Allan Ramsay, portrait-painter to George III.; Sir William Allan, R.A. and P.R.S.A.; James Archer, R.S.A., Francis Cruickshank, portrait-painter.

V. Navy.—Admirals—Sir George Hope, Sir William Hope, Sir Alexis Greig, Sir F. L. Maitland, Sir David Milne, Sir A. D. Y. Arbuthnot, Sir Charles Napier, Sir Richard Dundas, Captain Basil Hall, Captain Lord John Hay Lord of the Admiralty.

VI. Army.—Major-General Thomas Dundas of Fingask. General Sir Ronald Crawford Ferguson; General John Hope (Earl of Hopetoun), Lieutenant-General Sir John Hope Sir George Murray, Master-General of the Ordnance. Lieutenant-General Sir Joseph Straton; General Thomas Trotter, General Lord James Hay, Lieutenant-Colonel Peter Murray (Macgregor), Adjutant-General of Bengal Army. Donor of the "Murray Macgregor Medal; Colonel John Macdonald of Exeter, H.E.I.C.S., Donor of the "Macdonald Medal." This gentleman was a son of the famous Flora Macdonald, who rendered such memorable service to the Chevalier Charles Edward Stuart.

VII. Peerage, Civil Service, and Municipality.—The Marquis of Tweeddale; the present Earl of Wemyss; Earl of Camperdown, Earl of Cathcart; Princes of Orleans—Duc d'Alençon, Duc de Penthièvre, Prince de Condé Ninth Earl of Dalhousie, Governor of Canada; Viscount Melville, First Lord of the Admiralty, Mountstuart Elphinstone, Governor of Bombay, and author of "History of India," Adam Black, for many years Lord Provost of Edinburgh, and M.P for the city.

On leaving the High School, we approach an imposing range of buildings in the castellated Saxon style of architecture. This is

The Prisons.—The easternmost building of the group is the Debtors' Jail, which was erected in 1845-47; the new structure in the centre is an extension completed in 1885. The building on the west is the Town and County Jail, which was erected in 1817, when the Old Tolbooth in the High Street was taken down.—Opposite to the main entrance of the latter is a stair leading to

The **Calton Hill**, one of the principal attractions of the city. It stands 350 feet above the level of the sea, and commands a series of the finest panoramic views to be found in Europe.

"Traced like a map the landscape lies,
In cultured beauty stretching wide ;
There Pentland's green acclivities,—
There ocean with its azure tide,—
There Arthur's Seat,—and, gleaming through
Thy eastern wing, Dun-Edin blue ;
While, in the orient, Lammer's daughters—
A distant giant-range—are seen
North Berwick Law, with cone of green,
And Bass amid the waters."

Dugald Stewart's Monument, to the left, at the top of the second flight of stairs, was designed by Playfair, and will remind the tourist who has seen Athens of the "Lantern of Demosthenes."—To the north is the **Old Observatory**, erected in 1776 for an astronomical observatory, but now used for a self-registering anemometer, and rain gauge, in connection with the Royal Observatory. The building is interesting as having been erected after a design by James Craig, the architect of the New Town, supplemented by the celebrated Adam. Closely adjoining, on the east, is **The New Royal Observatory**, founded in 1818. It is an elegant Doric structure, from a design by Playfair, after the model of the Grecian Temple of the Winds, and consists of a central cross of 62 feet, with four projecting pediments, supported by six columns, fronting the four cardinal points of the compass. The central dome, 13 feet in diameter, contains a solid cone or pillar 19 feet high, for the astronomical circle. At the southeast corner of the same enclosure is the rectangular **Monument of Professor Playfair**, uncle of the celebrated architect of that name, near which is the unfinished

National Monument, the foundation stone of which was laid on the 27th of August 1822, by George IV. This splendid projected structure was to have been a reproduction of the Parthenon at Athens, and was intended to commemorate the achievements of the Scotsmen who fell in the land and sea battles of Napoleon's time. When twelve massive pillars had been raised at a cost of £1000 each, further progress was stayed for lack of funds. Viewed from a distance, the structure has a much finer effect than it could possibly have if finished.—A few yards to the south stands

Nelson's Monument, a circular turret upwards of 102 feet in height, with a winding stair inside, and battlemented summit. It was erected in 1815. On the flagstaff a huge ball is rigged, which, moved by mechanism adjusted to the Observatory, drops daily at one o'clock Greenwich time. Visitors are admitted to, the top, which is about 450 feet above the level of the sea, and the view from which is reckoned one of the finest in Europe, on payment of 3d. each.

Descending the stairs again we enter **Waterloo Place**. This approach to the city was planned in 1815 by Mr Archibald Elliot, the designer of the Prisons, and opened in 1819, on the visit of Prince Leopold, the late King of the Belgians. On the south side of the street is the **Old Calton Burying Ground**, where are the graves of David Hume, the historian, and Professor George Wilson, the chemist. On the east side of the centre walk of this cemetery is the Martyrs' Monument, a tall obelisk, erected in 1845 to the memory of several gentlemen—Muir, Palmer, Skirving, Gerrald, and Margarot—who were banished in 1793 for advocating Parliamentary reform. Almost opposite is the **Waterloo Hotel**, erected in 1819, at a cost of nearly £30,000, and which contains some very handsome rooms. On the other side is the Old Post Office buildings, erected in 1819, at a cost of £15,000, and now occupied as a hotel.

Passing the Regent Arch, and the Inland Revenue Offices on the left, we reach

The New Post Office.—This massive structure, which occupies the site of the old Theatre Royal, is in the Italian style of architecture, and was designed by Mr Robert Matheson of H.M. Board of Works. The laying of the foundation stone, on the 23d of October 1861, was about the last public ceremonial in which the late Prince Consort took part. The building consists of three stories, 66 feet in height to Princes Street, and upwards of 160 at the south end ; the front to Princes Street being 137 feet in length, and the façade to the Bridge 138 feet long. It was opened for business on the 7th of May 1866, and cost, including the site, £120,000.

Having returned to the point whence we started, we here terminate our first walk.

II.

St Andrew Square—George Street—Charlotte Square—and hence by Hope Street and Maitland Street to Donaldson's Hospital—thence by Manor Place and Melville Street to Dean Bridge—return by Randolph Crescent, Great Stuart Street, and Ainslie Place to Queen Street—York Place—Broughton—to Inverleith Row—and back by Henderson Row, Pitt Street, Dundas Street, and Hanover Street to Register House.

Leaving the Register House, and proceeding westward to St Andrew Street, we reach

ST ANDREW SQUARE.

Built about 1778, this was for many years the most fashionable quarter of the New Town. It is now, however, chiefly a mart for business, and is in this respect perhaps the most important street in the city. Some idea may be had of the magnitude of the interests at stake here, when it is stated that the liabilities (that is, the total sums insured) of the six leading insurance houses alone amount to over £45,000,000! and that their annual income is upwards of £1,800,000! a revenue larger than that of some States!

Entering South St. Andrew Street, the first building on the left is the **Young Men's Christian Institute**; and higher up on the right is

The National Bank.—Established in 1825.—With a paid up capital of £1,000,000, it has 76 Branches, and 1578 partners.—Adjoining is

The British Linen Co's Bank.—Established in 1746. This Association was originally formed for the purpose of granting loans for the encouragement of the linen manufacture of Scotland, but in the course of years it gradually developed into common banking business, and is now one of the first establishments in the country. The present building, designed by David Bryce, R.S.A., and finished in 1851, at a cost of £30,000, displays in front a series of six Corinthian pillars supporting an entablature, surmounted by six beautifully-sculptured figures representing Navigation, Commerce, Industry, Architecture, Mechanics, and Agriculture. The beauty of the interior—with its magnificent columns of Peterhead granite, its busts of celebrated Scotsmen, its lanterned dome of stained glass, and tesselated Roman-tile pavement—is in perfect keeping with the imposing grandeur of the exterior.. With a paid-up capital of £1,000,000, it has 55 Branches and 1080 Partners.—A few paces farther north, in a recess, stands

The Royal Bank.—Established in 1727. This building was originally erected about the latter end of the last century, as a town residence, by Sir Lawrence Dundas, Bart., who had acquired a large fortune as a commissary-general in the army, who was Member of Parliament for Edinburgh in 1768, and whose descendants are now Earls of Zetland. The bronze statue, in Roman costume, leaning on a charger, in front of the Bank, is that of John, fourth Earl of Hopetoun, who died in 1823. Under the name of Sir John Hope, he was a distinguished Peninsular officer, and assumed the command of the British Army at Corunna, after the death of Sir John Moore. The telling room of this Bank is a magnificent apartment, with a roof rising in the form of a dome, and pierced with numerous star-shaped windows. The Bank, with a paid-up capital of £2,000,000, has 85 Branches and 1321 partners.—Immediately adjoining is

The Douglas Hotel.—It was originally built as a fashionable mansion for a leading lawyer and somewhat noted character in his day, Mr Andrew Crosbie, a member of the Faculty of Advocates, and the original of Scott's Counsellor Pleydell in "Guy Mannering," who removed hither from his old residence at the foot of Advocate's Close. It is now the office of the Scottish Union Insurance Company.

On the north side, No. 21, is a common stair, in the third floor of which **Lord Brougham was born** on the 19th of September 1778.

The large and elegant Florentine structure at the south-west corner of the square, adjoining St David Street, was erected in 1848 for the use of the Western Bank, but is now occupied by the **Scottish Widows' Fund Life Assurance Society**—the largest Mutual Insurance Association in the world.

On the opposite side, in a floor of the corner house, entering from St David Street, but overlooking the Square, David Hume resided for some time, and died there on the 25th of August 1776.—A little farther along, on the same side, in an elegant Italian structure, is the head-quarters of the **Scottish Provident Institution**, one of the wealthiest and most important insurance associations in the country; and immediately adjoining are those of the **National Bible Society of Scotland**.

The Monument.—The tall fluted column in the centre of the Square, in the style of the celebrated column of Trajan, was erected in 1821, at a cost of £8000, to commemorate Henry Dundas, the first Viscount Melville, who was Lord Advocate for Scotland in 1775, and who afterwards filled several ministerial offices during the administration of Pitt. He was impeached by the House of Commons for embezzlement while he was Treasurer to the Navy; but was declared not guilty by the Peers. It is 136 feet in height; and the statue on the top 14 feet.

Leaving the Square on the west, we enter

GEORGE STREET.

It is one of the finest streets in Europe, and is 115 feet wide, and nearly three-fouths of a mile long. Although of comparatively modern erection, many distinguished persons have resided in it. Sir Walter Scott dwelt here, in the second story of No. 108, in 1797; in No. 92, Lord Jeffrey took up his abode in May 1810, and resided there for 17 years; and Lord Cockburn from 1816 to 1820. Sir Henry Raeburn, the distinguished portrait-painter; and the well-known Sir John Sinclair, and his talented and benevolent daughter Miss Catherine Sinclair, authoress of "Modern Accomplishments," also resided here, in No. 133.

The first noticeable structure, on the right, is

The Standard Life Assurance Company, the chaste Grecian front of which is surmounted by a pediment occupied by a sculptured group, by Steell, representative of the "Ten Virgins."—A little farther on is

St Andrew's Church.—This was the earliest erected place of worship in the extended royalty or new city, having been built in 1785, and is nearly circular in form, with a spire 168 feet high above a portico of Corinthian pillars; the spire contains the only chime of bells in Edinburgh. This church is celebrated as being the place in which the notable General Assembly of the Church of Scotland met in May 1843, when rs (all members) seceded, and marched out, with h at their head, to con- community which has ɔwn by the name of the

George Street, Sir Walter Scott resided for twenty-six years (1800-1826). He appears to have been very much attached to his residence here, as the following touching extract from his Diary shows :—" *March* 15, 1826. This morning I leave No. 39 Castle Street for the last time. 'The cabin was convenient,' and habit had made it agreeable to me. . . . So farewell, poor No. 39! What a portion of my life has been spent there! It has sheltered me from the prime of life to its decline; and now I must bid good-bye to it."

Bank, established in ling was erected in 1847, cture of a mixed Greek designed by Mr David portico in front has a umns being 35 feet high, road, and the pediment to the apex. The pedi- sal group of emblemati- :l of the late Handyside th a paid-up capital of :hes, and 1055 partners.

St George's Parish Church, on the west side of Charlotte Square, closes the vista of George Street. It was erected in 1811-14, after a design by Mr Thomas Reid, in the Græco-Italian style of architecture, at a cost of £33,000, and can accommodate 1600 persons. Its massive dome, designed after that of St Paul's in London, presents a most imposing appearance.

, on the right, at the :t, is the **Clydesdale** re of the roadway is the

Leaving Charlotte Square by Hope Street, and noticing, on the south, the beautiful Norman front of **St Thomas's Episcopal Chapel**, we proceed westward by Shandwick Place, and pass, in the latter street, on the right, **St George's Free Church** (Dr Candlish's), a handsome structure in the Palladian style, after a design by Mr David Bryce, seated for about 1250 persons, and erected at a cost, including £13,600 for the site, of £35,000. In Thomas Street, a little farther westward, the Show Rooms of Messrs Stuart & Company, Patent Selenitic Manufacturers, where there is a magnificent display of architectural decorations of all kinds, and also of concrete pavements, will well repay a visit. Proceeding still farther westward, we reach the **Haymarket Station**, now chiefly used as a coal depot. Some of the coal merchants here are amongst the oldest and most extensive in the town. The firms of Messrs James Waldie & Sons, and Messrs John Smith & Sons, extensive coke as well as coal merchants, have been established for many years; and their business ramifications have now become so extensive, that they have in operation a complete system of private telegraphs for transmitting orders between their various offices and stores throughout the city and suburbs.

) IV. by Chantrey. It ommemorate the King's 2.

the left are

Rooms, built in 1787, feet long, 42 feet wide, other apartments. The hem, was built in 1843, 10,000. It is a magnifi- long, and 91 feet broad, ɔdation for several hun- splendid and powerful

we reach another work **ue of William Pitt**, 333.—Still farther west, stle Street with George bronze statue of **Dr John Steell** has been

it's **House**.—A little reet, in No. 39 of which, a few paces down from

Proceeding along Corstorphine Road, and passing on the right **West Coates Established**

Church, designed in what is called the later pointed Gothic style, with a tower and spire 130 feet high, seated for 900 persons, and erected at a cost of £7500, we reach

Donaldson's Hospital, the most princely edifice of which the city or its neighbourhood can boast. This magnificent building, which was erected at a cost of £100,000, was designed by W. H. Playfair, and publicly opened in 1851. It is a splendid palatial structure, in the Tudor or Elizabethan order of architecture, with a beautiful chapel attached, and forms the monument of Mr James Donaldson, an Edinburgh printer, who bequeathed, at his death in 1830, the sum of £210,000 to build and endow an hospital for the education and maintenance of poor boys and girls —about 230 of whom are at present sheltered within its walls.—Retracing our steps as far as Atholl Place, we pass down Manor Place, where Mrs Grant of Laggan, the authoress of "Letters from the Mountains," and other works, lived and died, and enter, on the right, Melville Crescent, which contains a fine bronze **Statue of the second Viscount Melville**, by Steell, and passing along Melville Street, in the house No. 36 of which Patrick Fraser Tytler, the historian, resided for some years, we reach, by way of Queensferry Street, on the left,

The Dean Bridge, erected in 1832, after a design by the celebrated Telford. It is 447 feet long, 39 feet broad, rises 106 feet above the bed of the stream, and consists of four arches, each of 96 feet span. From the parapet a splendid view is obtained of the vale of the Water of Leith; and away in the distance the blue Forth and the hills of Fife. Far down in the ravine below, on the right, stands the Doric temple-like structure called **St Bernard's Well**. It was erected in 1789, by Lord Gardenstone, a senator of the College of Justice, who considered he had derived great and lasting benefit from the medicinal virtue of its waters. The design, by Nasmyth, was a copy of the Sybil's Temple at Tivoli, and in the centre of the upper portion of the structure there is a statue of Hygeia.—At the north-west corner of the bridge is

Trinity Episcopal Chapel, an elegant Gothic edifice, with square tower, nave, and aisles. It was designed by Mr John Henderson, and founded in 1838.

St. Mary's Cathedral has recently been opened between Palmerston Place and Melville Street. It was designed by Sir Gilbert Scott, and cost over £100,000. The money was left by the late Misses Walker, of Coates.

Fettes College, Comely Bank.

This noble edifice, situated in one of the most salubrious suburbs of the city, was founded by Sir William Fettes, Bart. of Comely Bank, and formerly a merchant and Lord Provost of Edinburgh, who died in 1836, and left the residue of his estate for the education, maintenance, and outfit of a limited number of boys whose parents have fallen into adversity through innocent misfortune. The number of boys to be admitted on the foundation, and maintained and educated in the College at the expense of the endowment, is not at any one time to exceed fifty. In addition to these, such a number of boys as the trustees may from time to time determine are received as day scholars and boarders, for whose accommodation several Boarding-Houses, capable of receiving fifty boys each, have been erected, and are under the superintendence of the Assistant-Masters.

The College and Boarding-Houses are conducted, under the charge of Dr. Potts, the Head Master, formerly of Rugby, and late Fellow of St. John's College, Cambridge, on the system adopted by the great English public schools, Harrow, Rugby, and Eton. Dr. Potts is assisted by an able staff of Masters, all of whom have either been Fellows or have taken their degrees at Oxford or Cambridge.

The education given includes English, Latin, Greek, Modern Languages, Mathematics, scientific and artistic instruction, and is in the full sense of the word liberal, qualifying the pupils for the Scotch and English Universities, and for Professional life. A number of valuable scholarships and exhibitions to the Universities are also provided, which are open to competition by all the boys.

The present Trustees are, The Right Honourable John Inglis of Glencorse, Lord Justice-General; the Honourable Bouverie Francis Primrose; David Anderson, Esq. of Moredun; Archibald Campbell Swinton, Esq. of Kimmerghame; Robert Dundas, Esq. of Arniston.

Farther on, on the left, is

Stewart's Hospital, an elegant and commodious building, displaying a mixture of the Scotch castellated dwelling with that of the latest period of domestic Gothic, erected in 1849-53, after a design by Mr David Rhind, at a cost of £30,000. The hospital was founded by Mr Daniel Stewart, who held an appointment in the Court of Exchequer, and who, at his death in 1814, left £18,000 for the purpose. It was designed for the support and education for seven years of poor boys generally; but has recently undergone some modification, the hospital system having been partially abolished, and the institution thrown open as a day school. For very moderate fees, pupils obtain a first-class education, and may compete for benefits worth £700. —On the west side of a road leading down to Bell's Mills from the Western vicinity of Stewart's Hospital, is

John Watson's Hospital, a large and substantial structure, with an elegant Doric portico, finished in 1828, after a design by Mr Burn. The founder was John Watson, W.S., who died in 1759. It maintains and educates about 100 destitute children.

The first road to the left, after crossing the Dean Bridge, leads to

The Dean Cemetery, formed in 1845, on the site of Dean House, which bore above the main entrance the date 1614, and was the family seat of a brave old baronial race now extinct, the Nisbets of the Dean. The cemetery itself—the grounds of which are most tastefully laid out, and contains some fine old trees, and a number of striking sepulchral memorials, one very beautiful one, on the north wall, from the chisel of John Steell, R.S.A.,—occupies a delightful and romantic site on the summit of the high ground overlooking the Water of Leith, and has associations of a most interesting kind. It contains the ashes of Sir William Allan, the painter; W. H. Playfair the architect; George Combe the physiologist; John Wilson, the poet, critic, and philosopher, and near him his distinguished son-in-law, William Edmondstoune Aytoun, author of "Lays of the Scottish Cavaliers," and other works, and for many years Professor of Rhetoric and Belles-Lettres in the University of Edinburgh, and editor of *Blackwood's Magazine;* and on the opposite side of the walk, his colleagues, Edward Forbes, the naturalist, and John Goodsir, the anatomist ; and near the west wall, Francis Jeffrey, and his friends, Lords Cockburn and Rutherfurd ; David Scott, the painter, and many other distinguished persons.

Leaving the cemetery by the western gate, and passing Bell's Mills and the village of the Water of Leith on the left, we pass along Randolph Crescent, Great Stuart Street, and Ainslie Place,—adjoining which is **Moray Place,** in the house numbered 24 of which Francis Jeffrey lived for many years, and died,—to St Colme Street, at the east end of which, on the south side, there is a **Monument,** in the shape of an elegant Eleanor cross, **to the memory of the late Miss Catherine Sinclair,** authoress of " Modern Accomplishments," and many other works.—A few paces to the east is

Queen Street, at one time the fashionable promenade of the town, and from which a very fine view of the Forth and the high lands to the north is obtained. On the right is **The Edinburgh Educational Institution for Young Ladies,** formerly known as the Merchant Maiden Hospital ; but which has recently been thrown open as a public school, where 1200 young ladies, for very moderate fees, receive a superior education, and may compete for benefits worth £700. Between Castle Street and Frederick Street is **St Luke's Free Church;** farther eastward, No. 14, is the **Caledonian United Service Club**; and adjoining, on the east, No. 9, is the **Physicians' Hall,** which was built in 1845, after a design by Thomas Hamilton, and is adorned in front with a double Corinthian portico, supporting statues of Esculapius, Hippocrates, and Hygeia, from the chisel of the late Handyside Ritchie. A few paces farther east is **Queen Street Hall**, and at No. 4, the **Philosophical Institution**, containing library, reading-room, and news-room, and to which strangers, members of kindred institutions, are admitted free. Further east is the **Scottish National Portrait Gallery**.

Passing eastward into **York Place**, where Sir Henry Raeburn, Dr George Combe, and Dr Abercromby, and other distinguished persons have resided, the first noticeable building is on the right, a few paces from North St Andrew Street—

St George's Episcopal Chapel, a quaint dingy-looking little edifice, in the Gothic style of architecture, erected in 1794, after a design by the celebrated Robert Adam.—At the north-east corner of the street is

St Paul's Episcopal Chapel, a beautiful Gothic structure, consisting of nave and aisles, measuring 123 feet by 73, and built in 1818 after a design by Mr Elliott, at a cost of about £12,000. The Rev. Archibald Alison, author of the once popular "Essays on Taste," and father of the distinguished historian, was incumbent here for many years before his death in 1839.—On the opposite side of the street is Broughton Street, in which is

St Mary's Roman Catholic Chapel, the principal place of worship belonging to the Roman Catholics in Edinburgh, and built in 1813, at an expense of £8000, after a design by Mr James Gillespie Graham. It has an elegant Gothic front, with pinnacles rising to the height of 70 feet, and contains a fine organ and a beautiful altar-piece.—Closely adjoining it is

The Theatre-Royal, erected in 1876, and embracing in its construction all the recent improvements for rendering theatrical representations in the most effective manner. The old Adelphi Theatre, which at one time occupied this site, was burnt down in 1853. The Queen's Theatre and Opera House took its place, but was also destroyed by fire in 1865, and again in 1875.—A little to the east here is

Leith Walk, which was originally a line of defensive earthwork, defended by a trench and a mound, and protected by a battery at each end, and which was constructed by General Leslie in 1650, on the approach of Cromwell to Edinburgh before the battle of Dunbar. When the war was shifted to other quarters, this mound became a kind of footpath, but after the construction of the North Bridge it was converted into the present broad carriage-way at the expense of the city.

Proceeding down **Broughton Street**, we pass, on the left, a plain-looking Ionic building, used as a place of worship by the Gaelic (Established) Church. Near to it, and forming the south-east corner of Albany Street is a Congregational Chapel; at the opposite corner stands

St Mary's Free Church, an important example of the Perpendicular Gothic style of architecture, the erection of which cost about £13,000.

Adjoining it is one of the elementary schools which the Governors of George Heriot's Hospital were empowered, by Act of Parliament, to erect from their surplus revenues.

Pursuing our way northwards, we pass, on the right, Broughton Place, at the north-west corner of which is **St James's Episcopal Chapel**, and at the east end a United Presbyterian Church, with a handsome Doric portico, erected in 1824. —A little farther northwards is a new place of worship for the disciples of Edward Irving; and about 100 yards farther on is

St. Mary's Parish Church, possessing a front of considerable elegance, and a spire rising to the height of 168 feet.

Leaving this, we advance to the village of **Canonmills**, with its bridge spanning the Water of Leith, on the left bank of which is a series of buildings in the design of a Moorish fortress, and erected in 1824 for an oil-gas scheme, which proved abortive. In **Tanfield Hall**, one of these buildings, the first General Assembly of the Free Church was held on the 18th of May 1843.—Proceeding northward to Inverleith Row, a short distance brings us to

The Botanic Gardens, originally founded in 1670, but the present gardens were only formed in 1822-24, and now comprise 27½ acres. They have recently been admirably rearranged on the most improved scientific principles, and the visitor will now be enabled to see at a glance the whole species of each genus planted in distinct and complete groups. The gardens also contain a Museum, a Lecture-room, a Herbarium, second only to that at Kew, extensive Hot-houses, Palm-house, &c. The Palm-House is one of the largest in the kingdom, being 100 feet long, 57 feet broad, and 70 feet high. There are several memorial trees here which were planted by the late Prince Consort, the Prince of Wales, the Duke of Edinburgh, Lyon Playfair, M.P., &c. There is also a very fine view of Edinburgh to be had from these gardens. The public are admitted free to all parts of the gardens every day in summer from 6 A.M. till 6 P.M., on Saturday (June, July, and August), till 8 P.M.; in winter, from daylight till dusk.—A little farther to the north, on the right, is a road striking off towards the east, which leads to

Warriston Cemetery, with its chaste little chapel, tastefully laid-out grounds, and numerous monuments, one of the most recent of which, and perhaps the most interesting, is that erected to the memory of the late Alexander Smith, whose remains are interred near the eastern gate. "It claims special notice," says a writer in the *Scotsman*, "as one of the most artistic and appropriate works of the kind to be seen in any of our cemeteries. It is in the form of an Iona or West Highland cross, of Binney stone, 12 feet in height, set in a massive square base 4 feet high. In the centre of the shaft is a bronze medallion of the poet, by William Brodie, R. S. A.—an excellent work of art, and a striking likeness—above which is the inscription, 'Alexander Smith, Poet and Essayist,' and below are the places and dates of his birth and death. The upper part of the shaft and the cross itself are elaborately carved in a style of ornament which, though novel in design, is strictly characteristic. For the design of this very striking and beautiful monument, the friends of the poet are indebted to Mr James Drummond, R.S.A.—a labour of love in which artistic skill and antiquarian knowledge have combined to the production of a work which is in its own kind quite unique, and commands at once the admiration of the least instructed." Here, also, lie the remains of Sir James Young Simpson, the distinguished physician, who—as the discoverer of chloroform, the subduer of pain—has been justly deemed one of the great benefactors of mankind.

Retracing our steps as far as Canonmills Bridge, and turning southwards, we reach Henderson Row, in which is

The Edinburgh Academy, an elegant Doric structure, erected in 1824, after a design by W. Burn, at a cost of upwards of £14,000. It contains a handsome public hall and library, and spacious class-rooms, with a large enclosed play-ground. Established by a number of distinguished citizens, amongst whom were Sir Walter Scott and Henry Cockburn, the institution was incorporated by royal charter from George IV., and is under the superintendence of fifteen directors, three of whom are elected annually from the body of subscribers. The teaching and governing staff, which has always been of a very high order, consists of a Rector, four Classical Masters, Masters of French, German, Mathematics, English and Elocution, Writing, Fencing, Drawing, Fortification, and Military and Civil Engineering. The Academy is divided into two schools—*the Classical*, adapted for boys destined for the learned professions, or who desire a thorough classical training; and *the Modern*, intended for those who are to enter upon the civil or military service, or upon mercantile pursuits. The complete course extends to seven years, and, in addition to special professional subjects of study, embraces every branch of knowledge now recognised as requisite for a liberal education. And although the institution is not yet half a century old, yet so excellent has been the system, and so able the teachers in every department, that it has sent forth some of the most eminent men of the present day—such as the Right Hon. and Most Rev. Dr Archibald Campbell Tait, the present Lord Archbishop of Canterbury; the Right Rev. Dr David Anderson, at one time Bishop of Rupert's Land; the Rev. F. W. Robertson of Brighton, one of the best, if not also one of the ablest men that have adorned the Church of England in modern times; Dr James Macaulay, formerly editor of the *Literary Gazette*, and now editor of the *Leisure Hour* and the *Sunday at Home;* Sir Colin Blackburn, one of the Justices of the Queen's Bench; the late William Edmondstoune Aytoun, Professor of Rhetoric and Belles Lettres in the University of Edinburgh, author of "Lays of the Scottish Cavaliers," of "Bothwell," and of a series of admirable tales and sketches contributed to *Blackwood's Magazine*, of which he was editor for many years; Sir William Dunbar of Mochrum, Bart., for several years a popular Member of Parliament and a Lord of the Treasury; the Right Hon. the Earl of Fife; and Mountstuart Elphinstone Grant-Duff, the highly accomplished M.P. for the Elgin Burghs, and Under-Secretary of State for India, and who was elected Lord Rector of the University of Aberdeen in 1866 and 1869.

The Deaf and Dumb Institution is a plain-looking commodious mansion, pleasantly situated within garden grounds, to the west of the Edinburgh Academy, and was established in 1810 for the board and education of deaf and dumb boys and girls. The funds for the erection of the building, about £7000, were collected by public subscription.

St Stephen's Church is a stately octagonal edifice, in a mixed Roman style, with a square tower 163 feet high, terminated at the top with a balustrade, and stands at the north termination of St Vincent Street, to the southward of the Deaf and Dumb Institution. It was designed by Playfair, and erected in 1828, as one of the parochial churches of the extended royalty, at a cost of £25,000, and can accommodate 1600 persons.—In the low ground immediately behind the church there formerly stood an ancient scattered village called **Silver Mills**, a portion of which is still extant.—In the low ground at the east end of Henderson Row, in North Pitt Street, is

The Royal Patent Gymnasium, one of the most interesting and attractive places of amusement in Edinburgh; and no stranger visiting the city should depart without seeing it, containing, as it does, some of the most curious and amusing gymnastic inventions ever seen. It was introduced here at considerable expense by its proprietor, Mr Cox of Gorgie House, for the purpose of affording healthful and exhilarating out-door recreation to great numbers at once; and was opened in April 1865 by the Provosts, Magistrates, and Councillors of Edinburgh and Leith, and a large number of the leading inhabitants of the city and county. Amongst the many interesting things here may be mentioned a "Rotary Boat," 471 feet in circumference, and seated for 600 rowers; a "Velocipede Paddle Merry-go-Round," 160 feet in circumference, and seated for 600 persons, who propel the machine by sitting astride on the rim and pushing their feet against the ground; a "Giant See-Saw 'Chang,'" 100 feet long and 7 feet broad, like a bridge supported on an axle, and capable of containing 200 persons, alternately elevating them to a height of 50 feet and then sinking almost to the ground; a "Self-adjusting Trapeze," in five series of three each, enabling gymnasts to swing by the hands a distance of 130 feet from one Trapeze to the other; a "Compound Pendulum Swing," holding about 100 persons, and kept in motion by their own exertions, with no end of Rotary Ladders, Vaulting and Climbing Poles, Stilts, Spring Boards, Quoits, Balls and Bowls. A very great source of attraction to youngsters is the Small Boats and Canoes on the ponds, propelled by various novel and amusing methods. There is also an Athletic Hall, with an instructor in attendance. The most recently-introduced novelty, however, is the Velocipede, with the largest Training Velocipede Course in Scotland. The charge for admittance is 6d.—under twelve, 3d.

Ascending the face of the slope southwards, we pass Great King Street, built in 1820, where Sir William Allan, the painter, lived and died; and, a little farther up, Heriot Row, in the house numbered 6 in which, Henry Mackenzie, the well-known author of "The Man of Feeling," spent the last years of his life; and speedily reach Queen Street, from which we pass, by way of St David Street, St Andrew Square, and Register Street, to the end of our second walk.

III.

North and South Bridges—Infirmary Street—North College Street—Nicolson Street and Square—Buccleuch Street—Potterrow—Bristo Street and Port—Charles Street—George Square—Buccleuch Place—Forrest Road—Lauriston—hence by Home Street and Leven Street to Morningside, and thence return by Bruntsfield Links and Meadows to Grange, and back by Meadow Walk, Forrest Road, George IV. Bridge, and Princes Street to Register House.

Leaving the Register House, and crossing the street, we reach

The North Bridge, which runs straight south, and was built in 1767-1772, at a cost of £18,000, and the roadway widened in 1875. It consists of three great central arches and several smaller arches, two small open side arches, and a number of small vault arches at the ends. The span of each of the great arches is 72 feet; and the height, from the ground to the top of the parapet of the centre arches, is 68 feet. The entire length, from Princes Street to the High Street, is 1125 feet. The average daily number of foot passengers traversing the Bridge is said to be upwards of 90,000—the number of carriages and other vehicles, upwards of 2000. The view eastwards and westwards from the centre of the Bridge, in a clear day, is very attractive.—Proceeding southward, and passing the High Street, right and left, we enter

The South Bridge, which was formed in 1785-88, and cost £15,000. The purchase of the old buildings to make way for it, cost £50,000; and the new building areas on it were sold for £80,000. Some of the sites sold at the rate of £96,000 per acre; and some even as high as £150,000. It consists of 22 arches; but they are all concealed by the buildings along the side, with the exception of the central one across the Cowgate. Some of the business establishments here are amongst the oldest and most extensive in the town, having removed hither from more ancient quarters in the High Street; one firm, indeed, dates its origin prior to 1638; another from the time of Charles the Second. Beneath the extensive premises of Messrs. James Middlemass & Co., clothiers, 18 South Bridge, may still be seen the fashionable dining hall of Bailie Stewart, a wealthy merchant a century ago. It is at present used by them as their laundry. From the railings on either side here, a glimpse is to be had of the **Cowgate,** a once fashionable and romantic garden suburb of the city, on the slopes of which stood the stately mansions of the noble and the wealthy. The street now, however, contains but little to tempt the tourists to descend to it—most of its antiquities having been swept away in the progress of modern improvement.—Proceeding southwards, we pass, on the right, **Chambers Street.** In this street stands the Industrial Museum of Science and Art (see next page), and also the Watt Institution and School of Arts.

On the left is Infirmary Street, in which was the first **Royal Infirmary,** erected in 1738 through the exertions of Lord Provost Drummond, to whom this city was also indebted for the North Bridge and Royal Exchange buildings. The Institution is now removed to Lauriston and the Meadows, and its site is occupied by the Fever Hospital, a public school and public baths.

The two ecclesiastical buildings opposite are **Lady Yester's Parish Church,** with a plain Gothic front, built in 1803, and a chapel belonging to the United Presbyterians, erected in 1822. The building at the foot of the street, facing westwards, was the **High School of Edinburgh from 1777 till 1828,** when it was sold to the managers of the Infirmary for £7500. The first High School was erected on the same site in 1578, and was used as such till the present building was erected. To this dull-looking place, then, for more than 270 years, the youth of the Scottish metropolis repaired for the acquisition of knowledge; and here the well-known Dr. Adam taught such pupils as Henry Mackenzie, the "Man of Feeling," Scott, Jeffrey, Brougham, Cockburn, Horner, and a host of others, whose names are known wherever the language is spoken.

The University.—It is a large quadrangular edifice, in what is known as the Græco-Italian style of architecture, extending 255 feet from north to south, and 358 from east to west. The entrance to the interior is in the east or main front, and consists of three lofty archways adorned with a Doric portico of six columns, each 26 feet high and composed of a single block of stone. Above this portico, which was originally intended to have been surmounted by a dome, there is a broad entablature containing a long Latin inscription. The original college, founded in 1582, by a royal charter granted by James VI., comprised a range of mean-looking buildings, consisting of an upper and two lower courts, surrounded by a high wall, and which were demolished in 1789, to give place to the present massive pile. If the plans of the original architect, Mr Adam, had been carried out in their integrity, the structure would have been much more imposing and magnificent than this; but as the erection progressed, funds failed, and a curtailment of the original design became necessary. This was accomplished by Mr Playfair, and in 1815 Parliament granted an annual sum of £10,000 for ten years to carry out the proposed modifications. The work of teaching began in the old buildings in 1583, under Robert Rollock, the first Principal. By degrees the fame of the College, and its long line of distinguished teachers, spread far and wide, and pupils from all quarters flocked to it. The number of professorships is now 45, classified into the Four Faculties of Theology, Law, Medicine, and Art, the latter of which includes literature and general science. Its early-won fame is still maintained, and, although the youngest of the Scottish universities, it annually enrols the largest number of students. There are 80 bursaries, amounting in the aggregate to about £40,000, apportioned to 136 students; and the aggregate yearly value of the fellowships and scholarships (all founded since 1858) is £1400. **The Library** of the University was originated in 1580; and the principal apartment —along each side of which are ranged marble busts of professors and distinguished students, is a magnificent room 200 feet long and 50 feet broad—occupies the south side of the quadrangle, and contains upwards of 133,000 printed volumes, and over 700 volumes of MSS, many of them of very great interest and value. (The Library is open daily from 10 till 1. Admittance, 6d. for single individuals, and 1s. for parties not exceeding 12. Visitors are conducted by the warder.) One very interesting fact connected with the University is, that the chair of Anatomy was successively filled for the long period of 120 years by a member of the same family—the three Monros. The family of Gregory occupies a somewhat similar position, no fewer than six of the name having filled academical chairs here from 1674 to 1856.

The Museum of Science and Art.— (Open *free* on Wednesdays from 10 till 4; and on Fridays and Saturdays from 10 till 4, and from 6 till 9. A charge of 6d. is made for admission on Mondays, Tuesdays, and Thursdays from 10 till 4). The building, which is still unfinished, is situated behind the University, with which it is connected by a small glass-covered bridge. It is in the Venetian Renaissance style, from a design by the late Captain Fowke, R.E., and will consist, when completed, of a series of courts opening into a great hall 260 feet long, 70 feet wide, and 77 feet high; the entire structure is upwards of 400 feet in length, 200 feet in breadth, and 90 feet in height, and is the largest public building in Scotland. "The great aim of the architect was to have every part of the Museum well lighted, and for this purpose a glass roof with open timberwork has been adopted, and the details of the whole structure made as light as possible. Externally, the front is constructed of white and red sandstone, and internally a more elaborate kind of decoration has been carried out. Altogether the effect of the building is light, rich, and elegant. In the evenings, when open, it is lighted up by means of horizontal iron rods in the roof, studded with gas-burners, the number of jets being nearly 5000!" The laying of the foundation-stone of this structure, on the 23d of October 1861, was the last public act of his late Royal Highness the Prince Consort. The principal apartments of the portion of the building now open are :—

1. The Great Hall of the Museum is a magnificent apartment, 200 feet in length, 70 feet in breadth, and 77 feet in height, the *Ground Floor* of which contains models and specimens connected with architecture, civil and military engineering, and collateral arts; the *First Gallery* and *Upper Corridor*, specimens illustrating the history of glass, pottery, and porcelain, ornamental metal work, wood-carving, the application of mineral, animal, and vegetable substances to ornamental purposes, &c.; the *Upper Gallery* contains a collection of food specimens, a colonial collection, and a number of raw products.

2. The Natural History Hall, or East Saloon, is 130 feet in length, 57 feet in breadth, and 77 feet in height. The *Ground Floor* contains a general collection of mammalia, the south end being specially devoted to a collection of British Animals; the *First Gallery* contains a collection of birds, shells, &c.; the *Upper Gallery*, reptiles, fishes, &c. In this hall is suspended the skeleton of a whale 79 feet in length.

3. The Small or South Hall is 70 feet in length, 50 feet in breadth, and 77 feet in height. The *Ground Floor* contains models and specimens illustrating metallurgy and various manufactures from metals in their different stages, as well as of pottery, glass, &c. A small fuel series is also shown; the *First Gallery* contains specimens and a few models illustrating the materials and processes of the leading textile manufactures, such as those of wool, silk, cotton, linen, hemp, jute, &c., felt, silk, and straw-hat making, leather, fur, and also manufactures from bone, ivory, horn, tortoiseshell, feathers, hair, gut, india-rubber, gutta-percha, &c. ; the *Upper Gallery* contains the collection illustrating chemistry, the chemical arts, materia medica, and philosophical instruments.

4. **The North-East Room** (above the Lecture Room) is 70 feet in length and 50 feet in breadth, and contains an ethnological collection, chiefly arranged in the cases around the walls.

In North College Street stood the **College Wynd**, which was anciently known by the name of "The Wynd of the Blessed Virgin Mary in the Field," and formed at one time the principal approach to the University. It was **here, in a house at the top**, now swept away, that **Sir Walter Scott was born**; the celebrated chemist, Dr Black, Lord Keith, and many other distinguished persons resided here; and here also Oliver Goldsmith took up his abode while studying medicine at the University.— A little to the west stood the **Horse Wynd**, where the Countess of Galloway, Lord Kennet, Baron Stuart, and other titled people formerly resided.—Still further west on the south side of the street are the **Watt Institution and School of Arts and the Phrenological Museum.**

A few paces south of the University is Nicolson Street, built about the end of the last century, on the east side of which, a little way south of Drummond Street, is

The Royal College of Surgeons, a beautiful building in the Grecian style, with a handsome portico and pediment, supported by six fluted Ionic columns, erected in 1833, after a design by W. H. Playfair, at a cost of £20,000. The extensive Museum, containing a valuable collection of anatomical and surgical preparations, may be seen daily, *free*, except Tuesday, from 12 till 4, and in winter, from 12 till 3, by applying to the janitor at the door.—Nearly opposite is

Nicolson Square, in a house in which the sixth Earl of Leven, Lord High Commissioner to the General Assembly for twenty years, long resided.—A little farther south, on the left—Nos. 38 and 58—is

The Blind Asylum, a most useful and deserving charitable institution, and worthy of all the patronage the public can bestow. The institution was first suggested by the celebrated Dr Blacklock and Mr David Miller, both of whom were sufferers from blindness; but it was chiefly through the active and benevolent exertions of Dr David Johnstone, minister of North Leith, aided by a subscription of £20 at the commencement from the celebrated Wilberforce, that the institution was founded in 1793. The first house was opened in Shakspere Square, which formerly stood where the Post-Office now is, and nine blind persons taken in; but the public patronage having rapidly increased, in 1806 the present building at No. 58 was purchased, and in 1822 another house at No. 38 was bought for the female blind. Both establishments are fitted up with every comfort and accommodation for the inmates, who now number 148 in all—34 females and 114 males. The females are employed in sewing the covers for mattresses and feather beds, knitting stockings, &c. The males are chiefly employed in making mattresses, brushes, baskets, mats, &c., and in the weaving of sacking, matting, and "rag carpets," no less than 18 looms being employed in this work. The sales of the above kinds of work for 1870 amounted to upwards of £10,000. The building has recently undergone extensive alterations at the cost of about £3500, an elegant new façade, surmounted by stone-faced dormer windows, and a handsome cornice and balustrade, having been added, with a large centre doorway, and on either side two spacious windows separated by stone pillars. In a niche above the doorway is a bust of Dr. Johnstone, the founder. In connection with this Asylum there was erected in 1876, at a cost of £16,000, a large building for the employment of blind females and the education of blind children. It is situated at the foot of Newington, is easily reached by the tramway car, and is open to visitors.

Still farther south, on the same side, is West Richmond Street, a little way down which, on the right, is the church in which Dr Thomas M'Crie, the distinguished biographer of Knox and Melville, preached for many years.—A little beyond Richmond Street, on the left, a large archway leads to Simon Square, on the east of which is **Paul Street**, where Sir David Wilkie first took up his abode on his arrival in Edinburgh in 1799, and from which he afterwards removed to a better lodging in East Richmond Street, and thence to a comfortable attic in Palmer's Buildings, West Nicolson Street. The latter apartment, it may be interesting to know, had been occupied for some years previously by Alexander Runciman, the artist.—Still proceeding southwards, a few paces bring us, on the right, to

Nicolson Street Church, erected in 1820, and where the well-known Dr John Jamieson, the author of the "Etymological Dictionary of the Scottish Language," and other works, preached for many years. It has a handsome Gothic front, with two octagonal towers 90 feet high, and a very elegant doorway.—Taking the first opening to the right, southward, and passing on the right **Free Buccleuch Church**, with its beautiful octagonal spire surmounting the massive tower at the main entrance, erected a few years ago, after a design by Hay of Liverpool, we reach

Buccleuch Church, an unpretending little structure, erected in 1755, at a cost of £800, but which has recently been restored and embellished at an expense of over £2000. It is adorned with several very fine memorial windows—one very beautiful one, designed by the present Marquis of Bute, and erected at his expense, to the memory of an ancestress of his, Flora, daughter of Macleod of Rasay, who lies buried in the small churchyard adjoining. Here, by the way, in this obscure and almost forgotten little spot, are the graves of Dr Thomas Blacklock, "the Blind Poet," whose timely and appreciatingly encouraging letter to Burns first drew him from his obscurity; and the celebrated Dr Alexander Adam, author of the well-known work on "Roman Antiquities," and for forty-three years Rector of the High School—the teacher and friend of Jeffrey, Brougham, Horner, and a host of other eminent men.

Retracing our steps northward, we reach, on the right, **Potterrow**, an ancient aristocratic locality, which, so late as 1716, contained the residence of the Earl of Morton. But it has other, and more interesting associations still. The first interview between Mrs M'Lehose, the

ALISON SQUARE.

romantic Clarinda, and Burns, her Sylvander, took place at the house of a Miss Nimmo, in **Alison Square** here; and here, also, Campbell the poet resided during his stay in Edinburgh, and wrote his "Pleasures of Hope."—A few paces south from Alison Square, on the left, there stood, on the site of the new school, a small court containing some antique buildings, bearing the name of **General's Entry**, and in which Viscount Stair and General Monk formerly resided, from the latter of whom it took its name. It was in a house on the first floor of an old tenement on the north side of this court that the beautiful and accomplished Mrs M'Lehose resided with her two children, and where she received the visits of the ardent poet, Burns. A little farther north, on the same side, is **Middleton's Entry**, also associated, singularly enough, with another of Burns's heroines, Miss Jean Lorimer, the flaxen-haired Chloris of some of the poet's finest lyrics, and the daughter of a prosperous farmer at a place called Kemmis Hall, on the banks of the Nith, and who, after undergoing many vicissitudes, and having for a time "had her portion with weeds and outworn faces," was seized with consumption while residing in Edinburgh, and after lingering for some time in loneliness and suffering, she died in September 1831. Most of this property has been recently demolished to make way for a new thoroughfare now in course of formation. At the south end of this new road is **Charles Street**, in a house in No. 7 of which Lord Jeffrey was born on the 23rd of October 1773.—Adjoining, on the south, is -

George Square, erected in 1776, and for many years afterwards the most aristocratic quarter of the town. "In my youth," says Lord Cockburn, in his interesting "Memoirs," "the whole fashionable dancing, as indeed the fashionable everything, clung to George Square." Here resided the Duchess of Gordon, the Countess of Sutherland, the Countess of Glasgow, Robert Dundas of Arniston, Lord Chief Baron of Scotland, Viscount Duncan, the hero of Camperdown, the first Lord Melville (whose statue stands in St Andrew Square), and his friend, Lord President Blair (the son of the author of "The Grave," and of whom there is a very fine marble statue by Chantrey, in the great hall of the Parliament House), who died suddenly at his house here on the 20th of May 1811, and had a public funeral to the Greyfriars' Churchyard, "with all the civic pomp that Edinburgh could supply;" the Hon. Henry Erskine, Dr John Jamieson, author of the "Dictionary of the Scottish Language" (No. 4), &c. The house No. 25 was long occupied by the father of Sir Walter Scott, who spent the early years of his boyhood here. The old square, with its pleasant trim-kept, lawn-like gardens, has still an air of antiquated grandeur about it, and retains, in some of its present residents, not a few traces of its former dignity and seclusion.—Immediately behind, on the south, is

Buccleuch Place, a somewhat retired, sombre-looking street of tall stone buildings, erected in 1780. In a house on the third floor of No. 18 here, Lord Jeffrey took up his residence in November 1801, when he began his married life; and here Sydney Smith, Brougham, and others met with him to project the *Edinburgh Review*. The large isolated tenement facing the south-east entrance to George Square, was built and used for many years as Assembly Rooms for the aristocratic denizens of this select quarter. "In these beautiful rooms," says Lord Cockburn, "were to be seen the last remains of the stately ball-room discipline of the preceding age." It is now occupied as dwelling-houses.

Returning to Bristo Street, and proceeding northwards, we reach Lauriston, at the north-east end of which stood the **Darien House**, erected in 1698 as offices for the Darien Company, a scheme that proved abortive; it was in the French Style, with the curious high-pitched roof prevalent in the reign of William III. It was afterwards used as a lunatic asylum for the paupers of the adjoining workhouse; and removed in 1872 to make way for the present dwelling-houses; and it was here, while an inmate of a more modern portion of this dismal abode to the south, that poor Ferguson the poet died.

A little farther northwards is **Bristo Port**, which takes its name from an extinct gateway in the old city wall which formerly stood here.

THE OLD DARIEN HOUSE.

The archway on the right, bearing the name of the Hole in the Wa', indicates the site of an ancient inn.—Passing southwards, along Forrest Road, we notice, on the left, the front of the **New North Free Church**, with projecting basement, ornamented with a small Gothic colonnade.—Turning westwards into Lauriston, our attention is speedily arrested by the noble pile founded by the jeweller of King James the Sixth, and known as

Heriot's Hospital.—Orders of admittance to inspect the building daily from 12 till 3, except Saturdays and Sundays, are obtained, without fee, at No. 11 Royal Exchange, High Street. The foundation-stone of this magnificent building, which is said to have been erected after a design furnished by the celebrated Inigo Jones, was laid on the 1st of July, 1628; but owing to the civil war, and other causes, it was not opened till the 11th of April 1659. The cost of the erection is said to have exceeded £30,000. It is a turretted quadrangle, in a kind of Gothic style, measuring 162 feet along each side, and has over 213 ingeniously-designed and beautifully-carved windows, no two of which are alike. Beneath the high central tower in the north front, an archway leads to an open court 94 feet each way, adorned with a statue of the founder, which the boys of the hospital, and the children attending the free schools, annually decorate with flowers on his birthday. The chapel, which is situated in the centre of the south front, and which was restored in 1836, is elegantly fitted up with dark oak, and adorned with some beautifully painted windows. According to George Heriot's will, the Hospital was for "the maintenance, releife, bringing upp, and education of poore fatherlesse boyes, freemen's sonnes of the towne of Edinburgh." At present about 180 boys are maintained in the Hospital. "They are not admitted under the age of 7, nor above 10; they leave at 14. They are taught English, French, Latin, Greek, writing, arithmetic, book-keeping, geography, mathematics, drawing, vocal music, and dancing. Those who manifest talents and a desire for the learned professions are sent to the University, with an allowance for four sessions of £30 a year; ten out-door bursaries of £20 a year are likewise bestowed on deserving students in the College. On leaving the hospital the boys are provided with clothes and suitable books; such of them as become apprentices for five years or upwards receive £50, divided into equal annual payments during the term of their apprenticeship, besides a sum of £5 at the end of their apprenticeship as a reward for good behaviour." The present annual revenue of this wealthy endowment is said to amount to as much as the executors of Heriot originally handed over—£23,000; and its surplus funds have accumulated so rapidly, that it now maintains thirteen free schools in different parts of the city, attended by upwards of 3500 boys and girls. By a recent resolution of the Educational Endowment Commissioners, the Free Schools are abolished and the whole institution remodelled.

The Royal Infirmary.—This magnificent building has recently been erected at a cost of over £300,000. It is constructed on the pavilion principle, the several pavilions being connected by spacious covered corridors.

East of the Infirmary, across the Middle Meadow Walk, are the new buildings in extension of the University.

Continuing our way westwards along Lauriston, we pass the **Vennel** on the right, where a portion of the old city wall, erected after the battle of Flodden, in 1513, may still be seen bounding Heriot's grounds in this direction. To the left,

TOWER OF THE OLD CITY WALL.

a few yards farther on, is **Archibald Place**, at the bottom of which is located

George Watson's College-Schools, formerly known as the Merchant Maiden Hospital.—George Watson was originally a clerk to Sir James Dick, a wealthy merchant of Edinburgh in 1676, and afterwards accountant in the Bank of Scotland, died unmarried in 1723, and left £12,000 for the maintenance and instruction of the male children and grandchildren of decayed merchants in Edinburgh. From 1741 till 1870 it was used as an hospital for the board and education of the foundationers. But in the latter year it underwent some modification, the hospital system having been partially abolished, and the Institution thrown open as a day-school. For very moderate fees, the pupils obtain a first-class education, and may compete for benefits worth £700. The building in which it is now located was erected in 1816, after a design by Mr Burn, at a cost of upwards of £12,000. Upwards of 1500 pupils are now in attendance at this excellent Educational Institution.

Chalmers's Hospital, for the Sick and Hurt. It was founded by George Chalmers, plumber in Edinburgh, who died in 1836. According to his will, the bequest (£30,000) was allowed to accumulate until 1861, when the present building was erected.

On the same side of the street, a little farther on, in Lauriston Gardens, is the **Convent of St Catherine**, and near to it is a Church belonging to the United Presbyterian body. The Roman Catholic **Church of the Sacred Heart** is in Lauriston Street—the street diverging to the right.—Still progressing by the main road, and following it as it bends towards the south, a few minutes' walk brings us to

James Gillespie's Schools for Boys and Girls, formerly known as Gillespie's Hospital.—The Institution was originally founded in 1801, by James Gillespie of Spylaw, a merchant and tobacconist in Edinburgh, as an asylum for respectable old men and women, and continued to be used as such till September 1870, when it was converted into a day-school, where the children of the common people receive a tolerable education for a few pence weekly, and are eligible to compete for benefits worth £700.— On the left of the entrance gate to Gillespie's Schools for Boys and Girls is

The Barclay Free Church—a rather peculiar example of the Venetian Gothic style, designed by F. T. Pilkington; and of which, as a work of art, Professor Blackie says, although "full of individual beauties or prettinesses in detail, yet, as a whole, it is disorderly, inorganic, and monstrous." Its elegant spire, however, greatly relieves the monotony of the surrounding scenery, and is discernible from many distant points. The expense (£10,000) of erecting this church was defrayed from a bequest for that purpose by a wealthy old lady named Barclay.—We now enter

Bruntsfield Links, a portion of the old Borough Muir, on which King James IV. assembled his army before setting out on his ill-starred march to Flodden. Here the citizens still play at the ancient national game of golf. Strangers who may be desirous of engaging in the game, will obtain the use of clubs and assistants, and every information, on applying at the Golf Tavern (Connolly's), which stands a little to the south of Barclay Church, and faces the Links.

The pathway striking off across the Links in a south-easterly direction leads to Whitehouse Loan, where is located

St Margaret's Convent, erected in 1835, after a design by the late J. Gillespie Graham, and attached to which is a very elegant chapel in the Saxon style of architecture, after a design by A. W. Pugin.—The road skirting the western margin of the Links takes us to Merchiston and Morningside. It was here, in the

Castle of Merchiston, a fine old chateau, with modern additions, that John Napier, the illustrious inventor of logarithms, was born in the year 1550, where he lived, and dabbled in divination and other occult sciences having no foundation in nature, and where he died in 1617.

Morningside is a pleasant salubrious village abounding with modern villas and elegant residences. Near the parish church stands the house in which Dr Chalmers died in 1848. The whole of this district was embraced in the Borough Muir; and in the wall of the public road on the left, almost adjoining the church, may still be seen the large "**Bore Stone**," in which James IV planted his standard in 1513, and in the neighbourhood of which he marshalled his forces before setting out for the fatal field of Flodden.— In the lower portion of the village is

The Royal Edinburgh Asylum for the Insane, one of the most efficient institutions of the kind in Scotland, and which has accommodation for 600 patients.

A little beyond, on the right, is the **New City Poorhouse** at Craiglockhart, recently erected at a cost of about £50,000, and occupying, with the ground for cultivation, an area of 36 acres. It has accommodation for over 2000 inmates, and is fitted up with every improvement conducive to health and comfort.

On the left are Blackford and the "furzy Hills of Braid," the scenes of Sir Walter Scott's boyhood rambles—

"Blackford! on whose uncultured breast,
Among the broom, the thorn, and whin,
A truant boy, I sought the nest,
Or listed, as I lay at rest;
While rose, on breezes thin,
The murmur of the city crowd,
And, from his steeple jangling loud,
Saint Giles' mingling din."

From the crown of Blackford, too, he tells us Lord Marmion surveyed King James's host "spread o'er the Borough Muir below," and, "when sated with the martial show," beheld with rapture the distant city as it glowed "with gloomy splendour red." Transfixed with the surpassing beauty of the view,

"Still on the spot Lord Marmion stayed,
For fairer scene he ne'er surveyed."

Blackford Hill has recently been acquired by the City Corporation as a public park. The new Suburban Railway has a station here.—To the north of Bruntsfield Links are

The Meadows, a fine spacious common, about a mile and a half in circumference, and once the most fashionable promenade in the city. "There has never in my life," says Lord Cockburn in his "Memorials," "been any single place in or near Edinburgh which has so distinctly been the resort at once of our philosophy and our fashion. Under these poor trees walked, and talked, and meditated all our literary and scientific, and many of our legal, worthies of the latter end of the last and the beginning of the present century." Previous to 1658 the space which they occupy was filled with water known as the Borough Loch; but having been thoroughly drained and laid out with walks, shaded with trees, the place now forms a delightful promenade.

On the north side of the west division may be seen Sunnyside House, the **Royal Hospital for Sick Children**; and on the south side of the eastern section is the **Trades' Maiden Hospital**, founded in 1704, for maintaining and educating the female children or grandchildren of craftsmen.—Beyond it is the tastefully-kept grounds of the

Grange Cemetery, where lie the remains of Dr Chalmers, Hugh Miller, Sir Thomas Dick Lauder, the second Lord Dunfermline, who was for many years ambassador at the Courts of Turin and the Hague, Dr Guthrie, Dr Robert Lee, and other Scotsmen once eminent in the ecclesiastical world.—To the east of the cemetery is

Grange House, formerly the residence of the gallant Kirkaldy of Grange; of Principal Robertson, the historian; and also, more recently, of Sir Thomas Dick Lauder, author of "Legendary Tales connected with Morayshire," and other works.—To the south is

Chalmers's Memorial Church, a Gothic structure of the Geometric period, designed by Mr Patrick Wilson, and erected at a cost of over £5000. The clergyman here is Dr Horatius Bonar, well known by his numerous contributions to religious literature.

Leaving the Grange, we return by Chalmers's Crescent, the Meadow Walk, George IV. Bridge, the Mound, and Princes Street, to the Register House.

INTERIOR OF THE TOWER OF THE OLD CITY WALL STILL STANDING IN THE VENNEL—ERECTED IN 1513 (SEE PAGE 56).

THE ENVIRONS.

LEITH.

[*It may be reached by train from Waverley Bridge Station every half-hour, or by tramway car from High Street, Register House, and Princes Street, every few minutes.*]

HOTEL—"The Baltic," 14 *Commercial Place (two minutes' walk from the railway station).*

ALTHOUGH the seaport of Edinburgh, Leith is a separate town, with a population of upwards of 40,000, and is a place of considerable antiquity, mention being made of it in a charter by David I., where it is called "Inverleith," that is, "the mouth of the Water of Leith." The principal approach to it is by the spacious street or road called Leith Walk; and the oldest part of the town forms a long irregular street, leading from the foot of the Walk to the shore. Previous to 1833 Leith was under the control of the municipality of Edinburgh; but since that time its affairs have been managed by a provost and council of its own. The town lies on very low ground, and is divided by the Water of Leith into two portions called North and South Leith. In South Leith is the Links, an extensive common, with a number of mounds raised by the soldiers of Cromwell in 1560 for the planting of cannon. It was anciently much used for golfing; and Charles I. and James II. played at this game here. Of the public buildings worthy of notice the chief are—the High School, at the north-west corner of the Links, a neat oblong building, with a small lantern tower, erected in 1806; Seafield Baths, at the eastern extremity of the Links, were erected in 1813, at a cost of £8000, in shares of £50, each shareholder, or a member of his family, having a perpetual right to the use of the baths. The Parish Church, in the Kirkgate, dedicated to St Mary, is a venerable mixed Gothic and Saxon edifice, built in 1490, and consisting of ancient nave and aisles, with a modern front and tower, the latter terminating in a beautiful Gothic balustrade. In the small burying-ground surrounding the church, John Home, the author of "Douglas," is interred. The Town Hall, in Constitution Street, was erected in 1827, in the Grecian style of architecture, at a cost of upwards of £3000. The Exchange Buildings, also in Constitution Street, opposite Bernard Street, a large Grecian structure with a handsome front and Ionic decorations, comprising the Assembly Rooms, and Public Reading Rooms, were erected at a cost of £16,000. The Trinity House, in the Kirkgate, appears to have been originally founded in 1555; but the present elegant Grecian structure was only erected in 1817, at a cost of £2500. It contains some interesting old portraits, and the late David Scott's grand painting of Vasco de Gama passing the Cape of Good Hope. St Thomas's Parish Church, a little above the upper drawbridge in Sheriff Brae, is a plain Norman edifice with tower and spire, built and endowed in 1840 by Sir James Gladstone of Fasque. The cost of the erection was £10,000. The Custom House, at the North Leith end of the lower drawbridge, is a commodious Grecian structure, erected in 1812, at the cost of £12,000. Leith Fort stands on a high piece of ground at the west end of North Leith, and, with batteries for the defence of the harbour and docks, has accommodation for about 400 men, with stabling for 150 horses. It is the headquarters of the Royal Artillery in Scotland. North Leith Parish Church, a little to the south-west of the Fort, is a handsome Grecian structure, with Ionic portico, and spire 158 feet high; it was erected in 1814, at the cost of £12,000, and has accommodation for upwards of 1700 persons. The living is one of the best in the Church of Scotland. North Leith Free Church, a heavy-looking Gothic structure, with lofty steeple, built in 1858-59, is also in the same neighbourhood. But the chief objects of interest to a stranger are the harbour, the shipping, and the extensive docks, five in number; the last constructed are the Albert and Edinburgh docks, east of the harbour, covering over 20 acres. There is also a large graving dock.—Leith has also Two Piers of enormous length, the east being 3530 feet, and the west 3123, and which form a delightful promenade. A small boat plies between their extremities at the low fare of ½d, so that the visitor may pass along the one pier and return by the other. A very fine view of the opposite coast, and of both Edinburgh and Leith is to be had from the ends of these piers. As the principal port on the east coast of Scotland, Leith is rapidly rising in commercial importance. The yearly amount of shore dues levied is somewhere about £30,000. The chief exports are coal, iron, spirits, ale, paper, and linen-yarn. The imports, principally grain and timber.

Newhaven.—(*Hotels*—"The Peacock" and Philpott's.)—It is reached by train to Trinity or Leith every half-hour or so, or by omnibus from the Mound every half hour. The village lies a little to the west of Leith, on the coast, and is chiefly inhabited by fishermen, who supply the Edinburgh market with fish, oysters, &c., and who act as pilots. About 200 fishing-boats belong to it. It has a good stone pier and slip, and was long the principal ferry from Edinburgh to Fife. In the fifteenth century the village had a chapel dedicated to the Virgin Mary, and was called "Our Lady's Port of Grace." James IV. had a dockyard here in 1511, and built in it the *Michael*, "ane very monstrous grate shippe," the timber for the construction of which nearly exhausted the principal woods of Fife. The village itself consists of a long straggling street, with numerous bye-lanes and courts, but the rising ground to the south is now thickly covered with fine villas and gardens, and forms an agreeable place of residence. The fisher people here, like most of the same class on the east coast of Scotland, are a peculiar race, whose occupations and habits tend to keep them separate from the rest of the community. They rarely intermarry with families out of themselves, and so preserve a peculiar cast of countenance and physical constitution. The women, inured to daily out-door labour, are robust, active, and remarkable for their florid, healthy, and regular features, as well as for the peculiarity of their costume and the neatness and cleanliness of their personal appearance. They are to be seen in all parts of Edinburgh vending the produce of their fathers' or husbands' labour. The village has long been celebrated for the excellence and variety of the fish dinners to be had in it; and is, on this account, a great resort of pleasure parties from Edinburgh. Few distinguished visitors, indeed, to the northern metropolis depart without partaking of them. They are to be had in capital style at "THE PEACOCK" Hotel (Mrs Main's), and at PHILPOTT'S Hotel.

Trinity is situated a little way west of Newhaven, with trains from Waverley Bridge Station nearly every hour; it may also be reached by omnibus every half hour from the Mound. It is one of the most agreeable suburban retreats near Edinburgh, and contains a number of handsome villas with garden grounds overlooking the Forth. Alexander Smith, the poet and essayist, resided in a villa a little to the west here for many years, and died in it. An elegant chain pier, 174 feet long and 4 feet wide, was constructed in 1821, at an expense of £4000, by Sir Samuel Brown, R.N., with the view of attracting trade, but the construction of the pier at Granton deprived it of all chance of this. It is now solely used for the accommodation of bathers, for which it is admirably adapted. The least depth of water at the lowest tides is 6 feet 4 inches—the greatest depth at highest tides, 26 feet —the ordinary depth, 17 feet. The charge for using it for bathing purposes, 1d. There is also a very good bath establishment here, where salt water hot and cold baths may be obtained at all hours of the day.

Granton may be reached by train from Waverley Bridge Station every hour or so. It is about a mile and a-half west of Newhaven, and is the principal ferry to Fife and the north. It has a large hotel, but very few houses. Its chief attraction is the magnificent pier, constructed at the expense of the Duke of Buccleuch, who is proprietor of the estate of Caroline Park, in the neighbourhood. Begun in 1835 and finished in 1845, it is 1700 feet long, and about 110 feet broad, and is sheltered on all sides by substantial breakwater bulwarks. There is a slip for landing and embarking cattle on each side, 325 feet in length ; and berthage is to be had at all states of the tide for ships and steamers of the largest tonnage. The entire cost of the construction, including the hotel, houses for the officers, &c., is said to have been about £150,000. The Queen and Prince Albert, on their first visit to Scotland in 1842, landed here. Boating may be safely and pleasantly enjoyed here within the west breakwater, where a boat may be had for 1s. an hour.

Portobello is reached by train every half-hour or so from Waverley Bridge Station, or by car from Post Office every twenty minutes. It is a parliamentary burgh, with a population of upwards of 4000, and a pleasant fashionable watering-place, about three miles east of the city, with the finest beach or bathing-ground in Scotland. Of comparatively modern erection, and consisting chiefly of handsome streets and detached villas in the midst of garden grounds, the town is well-built and airy, forms a pleasant place of residence, and is largely resorted to in summer as bathing quarters by visitors from all parts of the country. From 6000 to 8000 strangers annually take up their abode here for shorter or longer periods during the summer months. It is said to have derived its name from an old soldier or sailor, who had been at the capture of Porto Bello in South America by Admiral Vernon, having constructed a small dwelling-house here, and named it in honour of his old commander's exploit. A handsome Marine Parade has recently been constructed along the beach, which forms a cool and delightful promenade and lounge, and from which beautiful views of Aberlady Bay, the Firth, and the opposite coast of Fife are to be had. It has also an elegant iron pier, affording capital facilities for boating, and which forms a promenade some 1250 ft. long, with seats capable of accommodating 2000 persons, and a spacious saloon for the use of visitors. The sands forming the beach are extensive and clean, with a gentle slope eastwards, and are well supplied with bathing machines, for the use of which, with towels, 3d. is charged. Hot and cold baths of sea water are also to be had in an establishment adjoining the Parade on the west. At **Joppa**, which now forms a kind of suburb of the town, there is a mineral spring (Chalybeate) which is said to possess some medicinal virtues, and which occasionally attracts strangers.

Musselburgh stands on a spacious bay at the mouth of the Esk, about six miles south-east from Edinburgh, and may be reached by train from Waverley Bridge Station. The town belonged to the Abbey of Dunfermline before the Reformation, but the superiority was afterwards conferred by James VI. upon the Lauderdale family, from whom it passed by purchase to the family of Buccleuch, who are now its lords superior. The long suburb of Fisherrow, on the west side of the river, is connected with it by three bridges, one iron for foot passengers, and the other two of stone. One of the latter is very ancient, and is supposed to have been constructed by the Romans; the other, consisting of five elliptic arches, and forming the main road communication across the Esk, was built by Rennie in 1807. Between the town and the sea are the Links, where Cromwell had his camp after the battle of Dunbar, where the Edinburgh Races are now held—the race-course, constructed in 1816, being about 2400 yards in circumference—and where a silver cup is annually played for by the golfers, who constantly frequent the ground in great numbers. An elegant monument to the memory of David Macbeth Moir, the "Delta" of *Blackwood's Magazine*, who was a medical practitioner here for many years, stands a short way from the station, and consists of a statue 8½ feet high, on a pedestal 20 feet high. The village of **Inveresk**, which has been called the Montpelier of Scotland, and which stands on the site of an ancient Roman *colonia* or *municipium*, is a southern suburb of Musselburgh, surrounded and sheltered with woods, and abounding with elegant villas and beautiful views.

Duddingston is a pleasant retired little parish village, nestling at the south-eastern base of Arthur's Seat; and perhaps the best approach to it is from the south, by the carriage road which deflects from the Queen's Drive a little to the south-east of St Leonard's Hill, and which leads past the Echoing Rock, on the left, a rugged eminence giving off good reverberations to the south; Samson's Ribs, a range of lofty basaltic columns, also on the left; and in the valley beneath "the Wells o' Wearie," so celebrated in Scottish song; and, a few paces farther on, Prestonfield House, the seat of Sir W. H. Dick Cunynghame, Bart., where Dr Johnson spent several days when on his visit to Scotland. The pretty little parish church, situated on an eminence overlooking the lake, and the date of the original foundation of which cannot be traced, is of very great antiquity, and is supposed, from the structure of the interior arches and ornaments, to be of Saxon architecture. A beautiful semicircular arch divides the choir from the chancel. In the surrounding churchyard, "where the rude forefathers of the hamlet sleep," Gray might have composed his "Elegy," it is so retired, and so romantically situated, on ground sloping gently southwards to the waters of the lake. The loch is a small placid lake, covering a surface of twenty-five acres, and about a mile and a quarter in circumference, enlivened with swans and waterhens, and amply stocked with perch and eels. At the east end of the village is a two-storied tenement in which Prince Charles Edward slept on the night of the 20th September 1745, before his march in the morning to the conflict at Prestonpans.

Craigmillar Castle is a conspicuous and interesting old ruin embosomed among trees on a gentle eminence about a mile south of Duddingston, and nearly three miles south of Edinburgh. It consists of a square central tower of several stories, an embattled square wall, with round towers at the corners, the whole encompassed by a rampart wall, with the remains of a deep moat. The castle itself appears to have been erected about the end of the fourteenth or beginning of the fifteenth century. The battlemented wall in front was built in 1427, as appears from an inscription over the gate. It belonged for 300 years to the Prestons of Gowrton, but became the property of Sir John Gilmour, Lord President of the Court of Session in 1661, in whose family it still remains. John, Earl of Mar, a younger brother of James III., was confined in it in 1477, on a charge of treason. James V. resided in it for some time during his minority, when he fled from Edinburgh to avoid the plague; and Queen Mary made it a favourite residence after her return from France in 1561. A small apartment, 7 feet long by 5 broad, is still shown in the castle as Queen Mary's bedroom.

Dalkeith stands about six miles south from Edinburgh, and may be reached either by train from the Waverley Bridge Station, or by coach from 4 Princes Street. The Palace and gardens are open to strangers on Wednesdays and Saturdays, when the family are absent. The town, beautifully situated on a gentle eminence between the North and South Esks, has one of the most important grain markets in Scotland. On the north side of the principal street, the High Street, is the old parish church, erected in 1384, in the unroofed choir of which is the burial vault of the Buccleuch family, formerly that of the Earls of Morton, and some interesting old monuments. St Mary's Episcopal Chapel stands within the gates of the Palace at the east end of the High Street, on the right of the entrance, and is a handsome Gothic edifice, erected in 1846, consisting of a chapel and chancel, the former 70 feet by 30, and the latter 25 feet by 17—the extreme length, including the screen, being 105 feet. The **Palace**, the principal residence of the Duke of Buccleuch, stands on a knoll overlooking the North Esk, in the midst of a splendid park and pleasure grounds, upwards of 1000 acres in extent, enclosed by a high wall, and entered by three handsome gates. It occupies the site of the old castle of Dalkeith, and was erected about 1690 by Anne, Duchess of Buccleuch and Monmouth. It is an imitation of the Palace of Loo in the Netherlands, in the Grecian style, with wings, the front being ornamented with pilasters, and was designed by Sir John Vanbrugh. The interior is sumptuously furnished, and the collection of paintings, many of them by the first masters, is extensive and valuable. The entrance hall and grand staircase leading to the state apartments are spacious and splendid. General Monk resided here for some years; and George IV. occupied apartments here in 1822, and the Queen and the late Prince Albert in 1842.—**Newbattle Abbey**, a seat of the Marquis of Lothian's, stands about half-a-mile south of the town, and about half-a-mile north of the Dalhousie Station, in the midst of orchards and gardens, on the banks of the South Esk. It is a large square edifice of modern erection built on the site of an ancient Cistercian Abbey, founded by David I., and contains a large and valuable library, a collection of ancient illuminated MSS., which belonged to the former Abbey, and a number of fine paintings and family portraits.—About half-a-mile south of Newbattle, and nearly a mile south of the Dalhousie station, on the beatifully wooded banks of the South Esk, is **Dalhousie Castle**, the seat of the Earl of Dalhousie. It is partly a structure of the 12th century, and partly a mass of modern castellated additions, surrounded with beautiful gardens and romantic pleasure grounds.

HAWTHORNDEN AND ROSSLYN.

Directions to Tourists.—The best and most expeditious mode of visiting these two beautiful places, is to proceed direct by rail to Hawthornden, enter the grounds by the lodge there, and, after viewing the house and caves, proceed by a path up the south bank of the Esk to a postern in the boundary wall at Rosslyn, through which the Tourist emerges into the open ground beneath the Castle. After viewing the Chapel and Castle, he may then return to town either by coach or rail. The walk through the grounds of Hawthornden to Rosslyn, by descending and ascending banks and rustic bridges, beneath the shade of tangled trees and overhanging shrubbery, is one of the most beautiful and romantic in Scotland.

Hawthornden is 11¼ miles from Edinburgh by the Peebles branch of the North British Railway. The station is within a few minutes' walk of the lodge. (Admission daily—charge 1s. each). The house, the "classic Hawthornden," and home of the poet Drummond, is perched on the very edge of a lofty precipitous cliff overhanging the North Esk, which winds through a narrow rocky channel, covered with hanging woods. It appears to have been originally erected sometime during the 16th century, and, as a Latin inscription on the wall shows, was extended and repaired by the poet in 1638. On the south side there is the ruins of an old fortalice or castle of unknown antiquity, the abode of the poet's ancestors, and through which the house is approached. In the face of the rock below the house there are a number of caves shown to visitors, about which various conjectures have been formed. But the probability is they were made during the sanguinary wars between the English and the Scotch in the thirteenth century. During the contests between Bruce and Baliol, they were the hiding-places of the redoubted Sir Alexander Ramsay and his followers; and tradition points out one of the caves in which Bruce himself is said to have resided for a time—

" Here, too, are labyrinthine paths
To caverns dark and low,
Wherein they say King Robert Bruce
Found refuge from his foe."

The house itself derives its chief interest from having been the residence of William Drummond, the son of Sir John Drummond of Hawthornden, gentleman usher to James VI., an amiable and highly accomplished gentleman, and the author of some of the finest sonnets in the language. He was born on the 13th of December 1585, and died on the 4th of December 1649, and was interred in the family vault in the old church of Lasswade. Here, as is well known, he was visited by his friend Ben Jonson, in the winter of 1618-19, who walked all the way from London to see him, and sit "in Drummond's classic shade." The Tourist now leaves the grounds by the path along the river's side above described, which runs through the narrow and romantic glen that connects Hawthornden with Rosslyn, one of the most beautiful and sequestered in Scotland.

Rosslyn is 12½ miles from Edinburgh by the Peebles Branch of the North British Railway; it may also be reached by coach (7 miles) from 4 Princes Street. The village stands on the left bank of the North Esk, and now derives its chief interest from the remains of its ancient chapel (Open daily—admission, single visitors, 1s.; *bonâ fide* parties of ten and upwards, 6d. each. On Sundays, during summer, there are services at 12.25 P.M., and in the evening at 4.30 P.M.). The **Chapel** (or church, as it should more properly be termed) was founded in 1446 by William St Clair, Earl of Rosslyn, and was designed for a cruciform collegiate church, but was never completed, and now consists of a chancel and part of a transept. It is 69 feet long, 35 broad, and 40 feet high, and is divided into centre and side aisles by two rows of beautifully sculptured pillars, supporting elegantly ornamented Gothic arches, terminating in the grand and lofty roof, which is composed of a vast Gothic arch, divided into five compartments, remarkable for the beauty and diversity of their decorations. It is one of the finest and most interesting specimens of decorated Gothic architecture in Scotland, and, as a work of art, "may," says Britton, "be pronounced unique, and will be found curious, elaborate, and singularly interesting;" combining, as it does, "the solidity of the Norman with the minute decorations of the latest species of the Tudor age." It undoubtedly owes its chief attractions to the rich profusion of its mouldings and incrustations, and the marvellous beauty and variety of its decorations generally. As an instance of the variety, as well as beauty, of this wonderful structure, it may be mentioned that there are more than 13 different kinds of arches to be found in it; and every window, pillar, and arch, is distinguished from all the rest by ornamental workmanship of the most profuse and exquisite description. The pillar ornamented with beautifully cut spiral festoons is called the "'Prentice's Pillar," from a story that the 'prentice executed it during the master builder's absence at Rome, where he had gone to procure a pattern, and who killed the lad in a fit of jealousy on his return. The barons of Rosslyn are interred beneath the chapel, and were all buried in complete armour until the time of James VII. It was said that on the night preceding the death of any of the family, the chapel appeared on fire. Scott, in his beautiful ballad of "Rosabelle," alludes to this superstitious belief:—

"Blazed battlement and turret high,
Blazed every rose-carved buttress fair;—
So blaze they still when fate is nigh
The lordly line of high St Clair.

"It glared on Rosslyn's castled rock,
It ruddied all the copsewood glen;
'Twas seen from Dryden's groves of oak,
And seen from caverned Hawthornden.

"Seem'd all on fire that chapel proud,
Where Rosslyn's chiefs uncoffin'd lie,
Each baron for a sable shroud,
Sheathe'd in his iron panoply."

The Castle (admission, 6d. each) stands about 200 yards below the Chapel, on the edge of a precipice overhanging the rocky bed of the Esk that winds round its base. Little now remains of it but a pile of mouldering ruins and a triple tier of vaults. It is insulated by a deep natural ravine on the land side, and can only be approached by the narrow bridge that spans this gulf. The precise date of the erection of the castle has never been ascertained; but it was probably built about the end of the eleventh century. It is 200 feet in length, 90 feet in breadth, and the walls are 9 feet thick. In 1544 it was partly destroyed by the English under the Earl of Hertford; and in 1650 it surrendered to General Monk. In this old castle Earl William, the founder of the chapel, lived in almost regal state. He was served at his table, it is said, in vessels of gold and silver, by Lord Dirleton, as master of his household; Lord Borthwick, as his cup-bearer; and Lord Fleming, as his carver. His lady was served by 75 gentlewomen, of whom 53 were the daughters of noblemen, and all of whom were attired in silk and velvet, and adorned with chains of gold and other jewels. When travelling from Rosslyn to the family mansion in Edinburgh, which was at the foot of Blackfriars' Wynd, she was attended by 200 gentlemen on horseback, and, if after nightfall, by other 80 persons bearing torches. In the midst of the ruins there is a comparatively modern house, erected, as appears from the date over the doorway, in 1622.

"The Original Rosslyn Inn," here (or Hotel as it would now be called), is itself a place of some little interest to strangers, as much for its antiquity—for it is upwards of 200 years old, having been established in the reign of Charles II., in the year 1660, and is still in possession of the descendants of the family that originated it—as for the number of distinguished persons that have visited it. Here Dr Johnson and Boswell dined and drank tea together on the occasion of their visit to Hawthornden in 1773. Here, also, Burns and his friend Nasmyth, the painter, breakfasted when on a visit to the neighbourhood; and a long ramble among the Pentland Hills having sharpened the poet's appetite, and lent an additional relish to his morning meal, he felt so pleased that he honoured the landlady by scribbling on one of her pewter plates the following verses—

"My blessing on you, sonsie wife!
I ne'er was here before;
You've given us walth for horn and knife,
Nae heart could wish for more.

Heaven keep you free frae care and strife,
Till far ayont fourscore;
And while I toddle on through life,
I'll ne'er gang by your door."

Walk to Loanhead and Lasswade.—Should the visitor to Rosslyn be desirous of proceeding through the glen without entering the private grounds of Hawthornden, he may do so, on leaving the Castle, by descending a narrow pathway on the left, beneath the bridge, which leads through an open meadow, by turnstiles, to the woods of Rosslyn, on emerging from which, by a door in an old wall, he enters those of Hawthornden, and proceeds along a beautiful and romantic walk, winding through the recesses of the wood on the left or north bank of the stream, and from which a very fine view of the house is obtained. A short way from the house the pathway runs through an open meadow by the river side, and on through a wooden stile to the rising grounds overlooking the paper mills at Springfield and Polton in the valley below. Descending the hill on the left a footpath to the right is reached which leads to Polton Station, where the train may be taken for Lasswade and Edinburgh; the road to the left leads to the village of Loanhead, which stands about half-a-mile north of Springfield. Should the Tourist desire to visit Hawthornden House from this side, he will have to cross the river on the road at Springfield, to the right, and proceed till he reach the Lasswade road, where he turns to the right and goes straight on till he arrives at the entrance to the house. The village of **Lasswade** is beautifully situated in a hollow on the steep sides of a romantic part of the banks of the North Esk, and has always been a favourite summer resort of the citizens of Edinburgh. Sir Walter Scott spent some of the happiest years of his life here; and Thomas de Quincey, the "English Opium-Eater," also lived in a cottage here for many years, and in which he died in December 1859. Melville Castle, the seat of Viscount Melville, a splendid castellated edifice, erected about the end of the last century, stands about a mile to the north of the village.

Colinton is reached in a few minutes by the Caledonian Railway from the little roadside station of Kingsknowe, from which it is about a mile and a quarter distant. It is a beautiful little parish village, romantically situated at the bottom of a picturesquely-wooded dell, through which the Water of Leith runs seawards. There are some beautiful walks about the village, from which charming views of Edinburgh, and the distant island-gemmed waters of the Forth, are to be obtained. The little parish church—which, however, only dates from 1771—and the surrounding churchyard, are beautifully placed on a sloping eminence at the bottom of the dell, round which the stream runs slowly and with gentle murmur. Colinton House, originally erected by Sir William Forbes of Pitsligo, and the residence of the late Lord Dumfermline, stands on the summit of a beautifully wooded hill overhanging the village, on the south; Dreghorn Castle, a magnificent modern edifice on the north slope of the Pentlands, 489 feet above the level of the sea; Bonally, with its ponds, 482 feet above the sea level, and the residence for many years of the late Lord Cockburn; and Craiglockhart House (the hill is 540 feet high, and wooded nearly to the summit), the family seat of the Monros, the distinguished professors of anatomy in the University, are all in the immediate neighbourhood. Colinton was the headquarters of the Covenanters on the night before the battle of Rullion Green.

A little farther up the stream, on the left bank, is the pleasant little village of **Juniper Green.** Descending the banks of the stream behind the village, crossing a rustic bridge, and proceeding along a pathway through the fields to the south for a short distance, **Torphin Hill** is reached, one of the low heads of the Pentlands, and the view from which is said to be exactly that of the vicinity of Athens as seen from the bottom of Mount Anchesmus. "Close upon the right Brilessus is represented by the hill of Braid; before us, in the dark and abrupt mass of the Castle, rises the Acropolis; the hill Lycabetus, joined to that of Areopagus, appears in the Calton; in the Firth of Forth we behold the Ægean Sea; in Inchkeith, Ægina; and the hills of the Peloponnesus are precisely those of the opposite coast of Fyfe."—*Williams.* The **Pentland Hills** commence about 8 miles north-east of Carnwath, and extend nearly 12 miles in a north-easterly direction, terminating about 4 miles south of Edinburgh. Their average breadth is about 4 miles, and their highest peaks from 1600 to 1898 feet. The **Water of Leith** rises from some springs in these hills, about 4½ miles south-east of Harburn, and after a romantic course of about 15 miles in a north-easterly direction, enters the Firth of Forth at Leith.

Corstorphine—A pleasant little village, and favourite summer resort, is about 3 miles north-west from Edinburgh, and may be reached either by railway from Waverley Bridge Station, or by car and coach from the Waverley Stairs, East Princes Street. But as the Railway Station is a considerable distance from the village, the best mode of reaching it, for those who prefer a conveyance, is by car and coach. A pedestrian excursion to the village by the Queensferry Road forms one of the most delightful walks in the neighbourhood. By this latter mode of approach, the visitor proceeds along the Queensferry Road for about two miles and a half, passing on the right (1½ miles), **Craigleith Quarry**, covering an area of 7 acres in circumference, 200 feet deep, and which has been worked for the last 18 years, and then takes the first road to the left, which leads to the bottom of the hill, which is 474 feet above the level of the sea, its sloping sides covered with fertile fields, and wooded to the top with belts of waving trees. After a gentle ascent of about half-a-mile, a spot near the summit is reached called "Rest-and-be-Thankful," from which a series of magnificent views of the distant city and the surrounding scenery are to be had.

"Traced like a map the landscape lies,
In cultured beauty stretching wide,"

from the green slopes of the distant Pentlands in the south, to the blue waters of the island-gemmed Forth, and the lofty range of the Ochils in the north, and stretching far away in front to the towering cone of Berwick Law, and "Bass amid the waters." Ravelston House (David Davidson, Esq., manager of the Bank of Scotland); Craigcrook Castle, for thirty-four years the summer residence of the late Lord Jeffrey, and other mansions, are in the neighbourhood. The village, which lies on the southern slope of the hill, is reached by a pathway from this spot. The ancient Castle of Corstorphine, the family seat of the Forresters, of which few traces now remain, stood at the east end of the village. The Church, an ancient Gothic edifice, in the form of a cross, and dedicated to St John the Baptist, was founded in 1429 by Sir John Forrester, and is still in good preservation. Several altar tombs of the Forresters are in niches, the recumbent figures, life size, cut in stone. The males are represented in complete armour, and the females in the costume of their day.

Cramond is reached by coach from 4 Princes Street. It is a pretty parish village, about six miles north-west from Edinburgh, and stands in a romantic hollow at the mouth of the Almond. The site was anciently a Roman station. It has a small harbour, and an antique cruciform church, erected in 1656. Cramond Island stands about a mile from the shore, and is upwards of nineteen acres in extent, and is accessible on foot at low water. It was formerly the property of the bishops of Dunkeld, but now belongs to the estate of Barnton. Lauriston Castle, on an eminence not far from the sea, was erected in the sixteenth century by Sir Archibald Napier, a brother of the inventor of the logarithms, and at one time belonged to the famous John Law, of Mississippi notoriety. Cramond House is on the east of the village; and about a mile south from the Church is Barnton House, in the midst of a magnificent beautifully-wooded park, nearly 400 acres in extent, and which was anciently a hunting-seat of the Scottish kings. The grounds of Dalmeny Park may be visited from the village; and there is a pleasant walk along the beach to Granton, whence Edinburgh may be reached by rail.

South Queensferry is reached by a train from Waverley Bridge Station, and by coach from 4 Princes Street. It may also be occasionally visited by steamer, during the summer, from Granton or Leith. A very pleasant and interesting excursion may be made to this ancient, though somewhat decayed, royal burgh. It stands on the shores of the Forth, about nine miles north-west from Edinburgh, and derived its name from Margaret, the canonised queen of Malcolm Canmore, who crossed the Forth here on her frequent journeys between Dunfermline and Edinburgh. It contains the remains of a Carmelite priory of the fourteenth century. The small island in the middle of the Forth is Inchgarvie. Queensferry has been of repute in the past as the principal ferry on the Forth, and now has the distinction of being the site of the great railway bridge which is to connect the East and Midland Railways of England with the North of Scotland. A short distance from the station is the entrance to the grounds of **Hopetoun House**, the seat of the Earls of Hopetoun, and one of the most magnificent mansions in the kingdom. It is in the Italian style, and consists of a centre, and two large wings, and was begun in 1696, after a design by Sir William Bruce, of Kinross, and completed about a century later by the celebrated Adam. It stands in the midst of beautiful grounds, on an elevated terrace overlooking the Forth, the view from which is the finest in the kingdom, embracing Ben Lomond, Ben Ledi, and the whole stretch of country from Stirling to the mouth of the Forth. The grounds are freely open to the public. A little to the east of Queensferry is **Dalmeny Park**, the seat of the Earls of Roseberry, beautifully situated in the midst of fine grounds, with pleasant views of the Forth. The public are admitted to the grounds every Monday. A short way off, on the shore, are the ruins of Barnbougle Castle, till 1620 the ancient family seat of the Mowbrays. **Dalmeny** Village, about half a mile to the left of the highway beyond the park, is a pleasant, well-kept, little place, with a beautiful richly-sculptured Norman church more than 700 years old, but restored in 1816. It is reckoned one of the most perfect specimens

DALMENY CHURCH.

of Norman architecture in Scotland, and is supposed to have been erected about the beginning of the 12th century. It consists of a triple aisle, with a bell turret, and an apsidal chancel; and contains some exquisite specimens of beautifully ornamented interlaced Norman arches, and displays a rich profusion of fantastic sculptured decorations generally. A little beyond the village is Dundas Castle, the seat of the Dundas family since the days of Malcolm Canmore. The original square old Norman keep still stands attached to modern additions in the Gothic style. —**Kirkliston**, a village on the left bank of the Almond Water, may be reached by a short cut of a mile and a quarter through the grounds of the Castle. The church of the village is an ancient edifice, with a beautiful Norman doorway, and contains the old burying-vault of the Stair family, with the ashes of the first countess, the Lady Ashton of Scott's "Bride of Lammermoor."

Burntisland and Aberdour.—Reached by train from the Waverley Bridge Station, and by steamer from Leith. A very pleasant excursion may be made to this favourite watering-place, which, with its bracing air, and fine views and walks, will well repay the trouble. The town is sheltered behind by the Binn End Hills, a trap range of rocks, the highest of which is Dunearn, 695 feet high, and the Binn, 625 feet, to the base of which, and the ravines in the hills, there are some very pleasant walks; while the views to be had from these hills, and from the heights to the south of the town, of the Forth, and the opposite coast from Queensferry to the Bass, are romantic and beautiful. The parish church, erected in 1592, is a curious Dutch-looking structure, with an ill-proportioned tower. A little to the west of the town, overlooking the harbour and pier, is Rossend Castle, originally erected in the fifteenth century, and which was at one time the property of the celebrated but unfortunate Kirkaldy of Grange.— **Aberdour** is situated about three miles to the west of Burntisland, and is reached by a road behind the town, which forms one of the most beautiful sea-side walks to be had anywhere. The village, which is sheltered on the east by the Hawkcraig Cliff, and has a fine southern exposure, with its picturesque harbour, ancient castle, and wood-environed precincts, is one of the prettiest watering-places in Scotland. In the woods to the east of the village, a favourite resort for pic-nic parties, and on the heights to the north, there are some beautiful walks. Aberdour Castle, the seat of the Earl of Morton, is on the east; and on the west, approached by an avenue three miles in length along the shore, stands Donibristle Castle, the seat of the Earl of Moray, where "the bonnie Earl of Moray," renowned in Scottish ballad, was brutally slain in a private feud in 1592 by the Earl of Huntly. About a mile and a half south-west of the village, a little way off the coast, from which it is separated by a narrow channel, and for a visit to which a boat may be had at the harbour, is the little rocky island of **Inchcolm**, about a mile and a quarter in circuit, which was formerly the site of a Culdee cell, held in great repute in ancient times. Shakespeare mentions the island in "Macbeth," in the account given by Rosse of the defeat of Sweno, King of Norway, who had requested that his men might be buried there :—

" Nor would we deign him burial of his men,
Till he disbursed at St Colme's Inch
Ten thousand dollars to our general use."

It still contains the ruins of a monastery, founded in 1123, by Alexander I., who had been driven on the island in a storm, and sheltered by a hermit who resided there; they consist of a church, chapter-house, and oratory, of early English architecture.

DIRLETON AND NORTH BERWICK.

North Berwick—(*Hotel* "**The Royal**," *first-class, adjoining the railway station*)—is a charming and romantic little watering-place, 22½ miles from Edinburgh, on the shores of a small bay circling far up into the sandy plain, which forms a pleasant beach for bathing, and is reached by train from the Waverley Bridge Station. It may also be occasionally visited during the summer months by steamer from Leith. One very great additional attraction for fashionable visitors to this delightful watering-place is the splendid hotel accommodation it now affords. The "Royal Hotel," which stands on the brow of the hill, on issuing from the station, and commands a magnificent view, is one of the largest provincial hotels in the kingdom, and amply able to provide for a very large number of first-class families.

The visitor by railway may leave the train at **Dirleton**, one of the most beautifully situated rural villages in Scotland, about two and a-half miles from North Berwick; and after viewing the few objects of interest to be seen, may reach Berwick by a pleasant pathway. At Dirleton, embosomed among evergreens and overgrown with ivy, there is the ruins of an old castle, built in the twelfth century, and which was once the property of the noble family of De Vaux. The garden grounds in which it stands belong to the Right Hon. R. C. Nisbet Hamilton, and are open to the public on Thursdays; and as they are extensive and beautifully kept, will well repay a visit. There is not a lovelier scene than is presented by this village, with its fine green, its noble pile of ivy-clad ruins, and the distant rock-gemmed Frith.

Although **North Berwick** ranks as a seaport and a royal burgh, and its harbour is mentioned in records as far back as the time of Robert II., it is a place of no commercial importance. In the neighbourhood of the little harbour, which is dry at low water, there are traces of the ruins of an ancient church, called Auld Kirk, notable in the annals of witchcraft. On an eminence on the south side (the right) of the railway station are the remains of a Cistercian nunnery, founded in 1154, by Duncan Earl of Fife, and which Scott introduces in "Marmion," as the place where the Abbess of St Hilda tarried for a time to rest herself.

> " And now, when close at hand they saw
> North Berwick's town and lofty Law,
> Fitz-Eustace bade them pause a while
> Before a venerable pile,
> Whose turret viewed, afar,
> The lofty Bass, the Lambie isle,
> The ocean's peace or war."

About a quarter of a mile south of the town stands **North Berwick Law**, a conical hill 940 feet high, with a surface of 70 acres, and forming a well-known landmark, and from the summit of which, on a clear day, a splendid view is to be had. The ruins on the top are those of an old signal station, which was erected about the beginning of the present century, but which has long since been abandoned.

Two and a quarter miles east of North Berwick are the ruins of **Tantallon Castle**.

> " Broad, massive, high, and stretching far,
> And held impregnable in war "—

a once formidable stronghold of the Douglasses. It stands on a high rock overhanging the sea, whose "billows burst in ceaseless flow upon the precipice below." The only approach to it on the land side was defended by deep moats and high towers. It was besieged in 1527 by James V., who only obtained possession of it by treachery; it was finally demolished by General Monk in 1650; and is now the property of the Dalrymple family. An omnibus runs during summer from North Berwick to Canty Bay, from which there is a pathway round the edge of the cliff to the Castle.

Opposite Tantallon Castle, 2 miles off, lies the **Bass Rock**, or island, about a mile in

THE BASS ROCK.

circumference at the base, rising sheer out of the sea to the height of 400 feet, and inaccessible on all sides save by a narrow entrance on the south-west. It was a hermitage of a Culdee recluse named St Baldred, who died in it so far back as 606. It was for a time a stronghold of the Lauders, but passed to the crown in 1671; and the Castle, now in ruins, was, during the reigns of Charles II. and James II., chiefly used as a state prison for the confinement of the Covenanters. It was the last place in Scotland that held out for the Stuarts; and only surrendered to the frigates of King William on honourable capitulation, after doing them considerable harm. It is now remarkable for the vast numbers of solan geese that breed upon it. In June and July its rocky sides are covered with their nests, while myriads of other sea fowl obscure the air like clouds. The rock is best reached from Canty Bay, about a mile and a half east of North Berwick, where a boat may be had for 5s. or 6s. On Sundays, during summer, there are services at St Baldred's Episcopal Church here, at 11.30 A.M. and 6.30 P.M.

James Middlemass & Co., 18 South Bridge, Edinburgh.

OPINIONS OF THE PRESS

IN REFERENCE TO

THE VARIOUS CONTRIBUTIONS
SENT FROM THIS ESTABLISHMENT

TO THE

International Exhibition, 1862.

From "The Scotsman."

EDINBURGH CONTRIBUTIONS TO THE INTERNATIONAL EXHIBITION.—Mr. James Middlemass, Robe-maker and General Outfitter, South Bridge, has prepared for the Exhibition, and has now on view, a large and very handsome case (fifteen feet long by about eight feet in height), containing vestments of various kinds, including specimens of two departments—pulpit-robes and dress-shirts—in connection with which he may be said to have attained a national celebrity. Much more attention than formerly has of late years been bestowed in all sections of the Presbyterian Church, as well as other Churches in Scotland, to the professional adjunct of a seemly pulpit-gown for the officiating clergyman; and the frequency with which presentations of such articles to ministers by their admiring flocks meet the eye when glancing over the newspaper advertising columns, shows that these accessories are considered as important and desirable by the congregation as they can be by the pastors. Mr. Middlemass' case contains four pulpit-gowns, all of the richest material, and exhibiting the most exquisite and elaborate workmanship consistent with their professional character. They exhibit front and back views of two different styles of robe—the "Geneva" and the "Bishop"—the chief peculiarity of the former being in the substitution of "wings" for sleeves, as seen in the lately ubiquitous Highland Cloak; while in the second, the sleeves have the well-known "Bishop" or "gigot" form. We understand that the designs are quite original, and though we cannot pretend to much taste or authority in such matters, there can be no doubt that they have been highly popular, and have pleased most competent and fastidious judges. An explanatory card intimates that they "are exhibited to indicate the improvement effected in general design and workmanship, in conjunction with characteristic simplicity and elegance. They possess a special advantage in the adjustment of the Geneva wing and Bishop sleeve respectively, towards the back and balance of shoulder, by which the robe retains its position on the person, thus securing an agreeable wear." Perhaps the most attractive article in the case is a Turkish dressing-gown, or robe de chambre, a splendid specimen of what Cowper calls "needle-work sublime," requiring, we are told, nearly half-a-million stitches for its production, and altogether displaying a wonderful combination of luxury and elegance. Passing over "clerical dress suit"—in which excellence of material and beauty of finish are combined with economy in price—"Scotch Tweed Suit," "Clerical Overcoat," and various other garments, all exhibiting specialities and improvements in style, the eye is attracted by a display of dress-shirts, enclosed in massive gilt oval frames, and really forming very handsome pictures. Three of them are "model" shirts, exhibiting various improvements "to secure ease and comfort in the wear," and two others give a front and back view of a full-sized dress-shirt, beautifully got up, and showing a great deal of tasteful workmanship.

From "The Daily Review."

CONTRIBUTIONS OF MR. MIDDLEMASS, SOUTH BRIDGE.—Mr. Middlemass, Robe-maker and Outfitter, South Bridge, has prepared a very large and handsome case, furnished with a number of the articles for which he is most famous. The leading articles are a Presbyterian Pulpit-Robe, in the "Geneva" style, simple, of course, but elegant in their simplicity, and admitting a few chaste ornaments. Other two Pulpit-Robes are in the "Bishop" style, and present a fine contrast to the comparative severity of the "Geneva." A clerical ordinary dress-suit is also shown in West of England black cloth, as a specimen of what can be done in the way of beautiful finish, while preserving moderation in price. A clerical overcoat and summer

James Middlemass & Co., 18 South Bridge, Edinburgh.

coat which also form part of the assortment, are noticeable for improvements in style, fit, and workmanship. In the general department there is a morning coat, with a number of improvements in material, design, and workmanship; and also a Scotch Tweed suit, exhibited for improvements in style, combined with extreme moderation in price. One of the most attractive articles is a rich and luxurious dressing-gown, in the Turkish style, of the ordinary Paisley shawl material, but finished with silk and other material in a most sumptuous fashion. The remaining articles are all dress-shirts, with improvements in shoulder, front, wrists, collars, neckband, more numerous than we can possibly recollect. Every novelty in the construction is a striking improvement on the ordinary article, either in the neatness of the fit or in the comfort of the wear. They are highly finished, of course, and remarkable in that way as well as others; but the chief merit is, after all, the success with which the designer has secured convenience, comfort, and neatness.

From "The Art Journal."

PULPIT-ROBES BY MIDDLEMASS OF EDINBURGH.—In Class XXVII. there was a case that attracted much attention, from the singular excellence of both design and workmanship displayed in the production of its contents. This case, together with other objects all equally good of their several kinds, contained a group of specimens of Pulpit-Robes, manufactured at Edinburgh from the newest materials, and in a style that raises them to the highest ranks of works of their order. It is always satisfactory to us to notice whatever is eminently deserving, and particularly what evidently shows that thought and care, and sound judgment, have been applied with success to effect the improvement of an important manufacture. We have carefully examined the productions of Mr. Middlemass, and in consequence of the satisfactory impression produced by them, we have much pleasure in according to this case a place amongst our Notabilia.

From "The Courant."

Mr. James Middlemass, Clothier and Outfitter, South Bridge, sends a large case containing specimens of Pulpit-Gowns, Shirts, and various articles of Gentlemen's attire. The case is 15 feet long by 10 high and 3½ deep. Special prominence is given to the Pulpit-Robes, of which there are four shown on upright blocks to give front and back views of Gowns, made after the "Geneva" and "Bishop" styles. The Robes have been prepared from new designs furnished by Mr. Middlemass himself, who states that they "are exhibited to indicate the improvement effected in general design and workmanship, in conjunction with simplicity and elegance." The Robes are most handsomely ornamented and finished, and are examples of neat and substantial workmanship. Placed in the centre of the case is a very elegant Dressing-gown, brilliant in colour and tasteful in appointments. It is after the Turkish style—the material of which it is composed being Paisley woven. The Shirts are exhibited in four separate frames, and display all the "latest improvements" to secure the ease and comfort of the wearer, besides being finely embroidered. Specimens of improved Collars and Wrists accompany them. The other contributions of Mr. Middlemass are suits of Scotch Tweed and West of England Black Cloth, made in the most fashionable modes. Mr. Middlemass has arranged them to the best advantage, and their elaborate workmanship tends to make this case a very unique and attractive one.

BUSINESS RULES.
All Goods being marked in Plain Figures the Lowest Cash Prices, No Discount can be allowed.

Minors are expected to bring a note from their Parents or Guardians, and entire Strangers are also expected to pay Cash, or give a satisfactory reference when giving their Order, or P.O.D.

JAMES MIDDLEMASS & CO.,
WHOLESALE AND RETAIL

Clothiers, Robe-Makers, Shirt-Makers, and Outfitters,

18 SOUTH BRIDGE, EDINBURGH.

James Middlemass & Co., 18 South Bridge, Edinburgh

LIST OF ARTICLES
SUPPLIED BY
JAMES MIDDLEMASS & CO.
Clothiers, Shirt-Makers, and Outfitters,
18 SOUTH BRIDGE STREET, EDINBURGH.

Dress and Morning Suits.
Scotch Tweed Suits.
Overcoats and Ulsters.
Tweed Inverness Capes.
Velveteen Coats and Vests.
Dressing Gowns.
Railway Rugs and Bags.
Plaids.
Travelling Portmanteaus.
Ladies' Riding Habits—beautifully made and fitted.

Clergymen's Pulpit Gowns, a large stock to select from. Cassocks, Bands, and Hoods.
Lamb's-Wool and Merino Underclothing, the best Makes.
Umbrellas, Gloves, and Braces.
Waterproof Coats and Leggings.

Hats and Caps.
White Dress Shirts.
Coloured Flannel Shirts.
Oxford or Gauze Cotton Shirts.
Coloured Cambric Shirts.
Stout Night Shirts.
Boys' Shirts—all sizes.
Linen Collars—all sizes.
Handkerchiefs, Neckties and Scarfs, &c.

The Cutting and Making-up Departments are under the most efficient management, and every garment is warranted a satisfactory fit.

Inspection is respectfully invited.

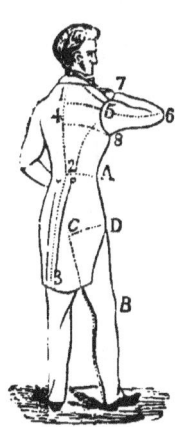

DIRECTIONS FOR SELF-MEASUREMENT

For Coat.—From 1 to 2 and on to 3 for full length; from 4 to 5 for breadth of back, to 6 for elbow point, and on to 7 for length of sleeve; round the arm at 5, 6, and 7 for width of sleeve; round the breast at 8, and waist at 2.

Vest.—From 1 over shoulder to vest length in front, with breast and waist measure as above.

Trousers.—Outside seam from A B and on to bottom, and also exact length of inside seam from C to bottom; round the waist at A; round the seat at D; leg at B, and also at bottom. Measure taken exactly by an inch-tape will insure a correct fit. The gentleman to mention if he wears his clothes tight or easy.

Measurement for Shirts.—In addition to the above give *width of neck* and *wrist-band*, and *height of person*.

STRANGERS VISITING EDINBURGH

CAN at all times be furnished with every description of GENTLEMEN'S CLOTHING, SHIRTS, and GENERAL OUTFITTINGS, in the Best Style, Best Value, and on the Shortest Notice. Gentlemen are invited to look through the Private Show and Fitting Rooms, whether with a view to immediate business or not; and as stating prices is no *Real Test* of the true value of an article, the *best* test is a *trial*, and the Subscribers have great confidence in recommending their present Stock for the inspection of visitors.

THE FIT AND STYLE OF EVERY GARMENT GUARANTEED.

James Middlemass & Co., 18 South Bridge, Edinburgh.

LETTER from Professor JOHN FOSTER, Union College, Schenectady, N.Y.

Dec. 31, 1875.

JAMES MIDDLEMASS & Co.,

It seems to me a duty to give some expression to my great satisfaction with the garments furnished me by you on two different occasions. The Tweed Trousers and Vest made in Oct. 1874, I have worn most of the time since that date, and they are still in good condition. The cloth of which they are made is undoubtedly the lineal descendant of that "gude braidclaith" which alone saved Bailie Nicol Jarvie, when helplessly dangling from the thornbush in Rob Roy's country, from slumbering with his "father the deacon." There is every reason to believe that the full supply of clothing from the same source as that already alluded to, and which came home with me last September, will do equal and even *better* service.

I shall take great pleasure in advising any of my friends who may be going abroad, and who may wish to see an unrivalled stock of Cloths, and to have them promptly and thoroughly made up, to visit the Outfitting Establishment of JAMES MIDDLEMASS & Co. After inspecting the shops of London and Paris, they will probably, like me, repeat that visit.

Yours truly,

JOHN FOSTER.

James Middlemass & Co., 18 South Bridge, **Edinburgh.**

LETTER from Rev. S. D. PHELPS, Newhaven, Conn., U.S.

21st *April*, 1874.

JAMES MIDDLEMASS, Esq., Edinbro'.

DEAR SIR,—I have for a long time been intending to write you and tell you how much I have been pleased with the garments you made for me.

The Business Suit of Prince of Wales West England Cloth, I think you called it, blue shade, I have worn almost constantly for nearly two years, and there is not a break in it yet, nor has it faded at all. It still looks well, and will last, I think, another year.

The Dress Suit—West England Broadcloth Coat and Vest, and Doeskin Trousers—is still looking about as good as new, and will do service another year as the best Suit. My wife says I never had a Suit that fitted me so well.

The Overcoat—a Waterproof—has served admirably, and is still good. I wish I had got a Heavy Overcoat of you.

The Shirts I am still wearing, and have liked them very much. Wish I had a larger number of them.

If well, and prospered, I hope to visit you again next year and get new supplies.

I can afford to pay the ocean passages, and get Clothes of you better than to have them made here. I have taken pleasure in speaking of your Establishment to friends, giving them your Pamphlet, Address, &c., and shall do so still.

Possibly you may sometime see a company of us coming to your place to get a stock of garments, &c.

Yours very truly,

S. D. PHELPS.

James Middlemass & Co., 18 South Bridge, Edinburgh.

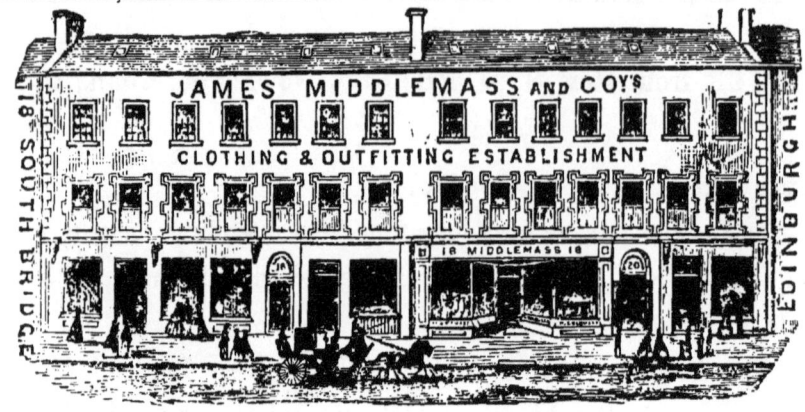

MESSRS. JAMES MIDDLEMASS & CO.,
Clothiers, Shirt-Makers, Pulpit-Robe Makers, and General Outfitters,
18 SOUTH BRIDGE, EDINBURGH,

TAKE the present opportunity of thanking the large circle of their Customers, throughout Great Britain and the Colonies, for the share of patronage with which their Establishment has been honoured for a long series of years, and which, they believe, has rendered it one of the best known and most extensive Establishments in the country for the manufacture of ECCLESIASTICAL, ACADEMICAL, and FORENSIC ROBES, and for GENERAL OUTFITTING for home and abroad. No efforts shall be wanting on their part to continue and extend the connection they have acquired, by rendering their Establishment, if possible, still more worthy of public support. Their customers can at all times have to select from a large and varied Stock of materials for GOWNS, CLOTHING, and SHIRTS, and will find their professional skill and wide experience such as to ensure excellence in FIT, STYLE, and WORKMANSHIP. In reference to this they have much pleasure in referring to numerous Testimonials from their Patrons and the Press (see other Advertisement Pages) as to the elegance of design, and beauty of finish, of several of their most admired improvements in ROBES and DRESS. (See also Directions for Self-Measurement.)

JAMES MIDDLEMASS & CO.,
18 SOUTH BRIDGE, EDINBURGH.

All goods are marked in plain figures the lowest Cash prices, from which no discount can be allowed.

www.ingramcontent.com/pod-product-compliance
Lightning Source LLC
Chambersburg PA
CBHW032249080426
42735CB00008B/1071